THE DIVING EAGLE

By the same author

THE KG 200 STORY: The True Story

The Diving Eagle

A Ju 88 Pilot's Diary

PETER W. STAHL

Translated by
Alex Vanags-Baginskis

WILLIAM KIMBER · LONDON

First published in Great Britain in 1984 by
WILLIAM KIMBER & CO. LIMITED
100 Jermyn Street, London, SW1Y 6EE

© Motorbuch Verlag und
Verlagshaus Paul Pietsch GmbH & Co KG, 1978
© English translation, William Kimber & Co Ltd, 1984

ISBN 0-7183-0509-4

Originally published in Germany in 1978 by
Motorbuch Verlag, Stuttgart as part of
Kampfflieger Zwischen Eismeer und Sahara

Photographs: Benno Wundshammer, Carlo Demand,
Dornier GmbH, Kenneth Wakefield, Richard Frodl, Siegfried
Geisler, Sepp Guggenmos, Pilot Press Ltd and P.W. Stahl.

Photoset in North Wales by
Derek Doyle & Associates, Mold, Clwyd
and printed in Great Britain by
Redwood Burn Limited, Trowbridge, Wilts.

Contents

List of Illustrations

PROLOGUE

I did not really want to believe it, but as an experienced weather observation pilot I should have known what to expect when clouds start growing thicker on the horizon – in this case the political one. In those July and August days of 1939 there was a lot of talk about the threat of war.

However, I have always been an incorrigible optimist, and in those days I had every reason to be one. Our small house at Deep in Pomerania, close to the waters to the Baltic Sea, seemed to be on another planet. I was young, newly married and, as a civilian test-pilot, had a dream job. Life was indescribably beautiful.

The morning of 1 September 1939 began like any other day. I was supposed to fly to Berlin and would have been back home by early afternoon. In fact, I was already imagining how I would use the time, arriving home earlier than expected, and after cheekily sounding the horn, I would stand at the door waiting for her welcoming kiss, with both hands behind my back, hiding some small trifle I had picked up in Berlin: 'Left or right?'

I can still see it all before me, the way it happened. I switch on the radio to check the correct time: instead there is martial music – or, as *she* calls it, 'catastrophe music'. And then it comes:

'Attention, attention! The German radio service will now transmit a statement that our Führer broadcast to the world at six o'clock this morning!'

We look at each other, and I put down my spoon (I was just about to crack an egg – boiled for exactly 3 minutes and 20 seconds, the way I like it). A declaration to the world? Finally, after a long preamble, comes the fateful sentence:

'Since five o'clock this morning, enemy fire has been returned!' ...

My young wife has suddenly gone deathly pale, right to the roots of her hair, and her question hangs heavy in the room: 'That means we are at war?' ...

My legs have grown heavy as lead, and I've lost all my taste for breakfast. Could it really be? Somehow I still cannot quite believe it.

And indeed nothing much happened that day. I flew to Berlin as intended, came back on time, was pleased about the little present I had brought back with me and, as usual, we both went swimming in the sea.

That was the day the war began.

A short while ago I happened to come across my old diary again, and can see that young self of mine before me. At times he seems almost like a stranger, but it was a picture of a young man who, without any desire on his own part, was put on this awkward and miserable old jade called 'war' and who – naturally – tried very hard to ensure he did not fall off. To say this ride was always great fun for him would be going too far. But that is how it all began.

CHAPTER ONE

The Reality is Different

And so civilians like us are all stuck in uniform, and I become a reserve Unteroffizier (corporal).*

My first task is that of a blind-flying instructor, introducing young airmen and officers into the mysteries of bad weather and night flying. That involves navigation flights with a group of such pupils in a big Ju 52 around Greater Germany, always around and around, and I hardly get more any home. It is the same over and over again, enough to drive one round the bend.

Should I pull a few strings at the State Air Ministry (RLM) to get out of this boring routine? Why not? And so I did, but three months went by before anything happened, then, finally:

9 December 1939
In my logbook I read the following entry: 'Ju 52 D-AHAF: Blind flight test. Take-off 1040 hrs; landing 1400 hrs.'

And that ends my dull rôle as a blind flying instructor. The transfer orders are already waiting for me when we land: 'Report to Ergänzungs-Kampfgruppe 3 (Training and Replacement Bomber Group) at Krakau on 15 January 1940.'

So much for my dreams of becoming a fighter pilot, but it had to be expected. They would not let such 'old hands' with all kinds of flying proficiency certificates join the fighter boys – they were needed more urgently somewhere else.

---

* It may seem strange to British or American readers that an experienced test pilot would not be commissioned. In fact, the Luftwaffe had many NCO aircrew, including pilots, throughout the war and promotion to officer status from the ranks remained highly selective until the very end.

The nearer the big day comes, the more we puzzled about what the future would bring. Some of us say they're afraid of being too late for any action, but are they really honest? I cannot get rid of the suspicion that quite a few of my friends would prefer a quiet and peaceful life as a civilian in the German Reich to this existence in uniform. Except the 'aces' of course – and there will always be some. Or could it be just my envy?

10 February 1940

Krakau turns out to be an utter disappointment. Too much stupid bull all around. I had imagined these training and replacement units somewhat different, and the experience was not pleasant to say the least. But perhaps Krakau might be one of a few dud places and I just had the bad luck to land there, who knows?

For one thing, hardly any flying takes place here. The Admin personnel, both officers and NCOs, have no idea about flying and just fill out Luftwaffe uniforms. My first impression is of much clumsiness, arrogance, laziness and shirking of duty.

As usual, where a group of men are gathered together in uniform there are some odd characters who stand out. Here we have a certain reserve Feldwebel (sergeant), in civvy street a Nazi Party District Leader* somewhere or other. He has taken on the task of giving political instructions, and unwittingly provides much merriment to us all by his misinterpretation of foreign words. The other day he made the following striking pronouncement: 'The misfortune of this war is the sole fault of the plutocrats! That word alone explained it all: *B*lutocrat, from the word '*Blut*' (blood)!' So now we know!

One bright spot in this otherwise miserable place is meeting an acquaintance in 1. Staffel (Squadron), Leo Krantz, who only a few short weeks ago had been one of my pupils on a blind-flying course. But there was much more to it than that.

He arrived in our training school at Rerik as an ordinary Flieger (airman), the lowest service rank the Luftwaffe could bestow, and yet he was a pilot of some standing. Naturally, we were curious and

* Gauleiter.

wondered about this because an ordinary airman would not normally have the necessary qualifications to fly multi-engined aircraft. Something was odd somewhere! And then we found out.

Apparently not so long ago Leo Krantz had been an Oberleutnant (Flying Officer), and a Staffelkapitän (squadron commander), no less. From what we learned about him I was convinced he was a good officer – and yet he had been degraded. What happened to Leo Krantz is all too typical of the times.

One day a few soldiers and NCOs of his Staffel had requested 'town leave' to attend some event organised by the Hitler Youth. As commander of the unit Leo had turned down this request, because service matters came first. A few days later he had a visit: the local Hitler Youth Bannführer ('regimental commander') wanted to 'inform himself' why the soldiers in question had been prevented from attending the event.

The way this young man carried on, and his whole self-important attitude were too much for Leo, and he ordered the duty Unteroffizier to throw the 'Herr Bannführer' out. Result: an official complaint via the Party channels, with a subsequent investigation against Leo, and then a court martial. It was quite a sensational case. Leo had several prominent character witnesses and advocates, including General Milch, but to no avail. The arm of the Nazi Party was longer and stronger, and Leo was sentenced to be reduced to ranks and discharged from the armed forces.

The war began in the meantime and Leo, who had already made preparations to emigrate to Chile, volunteered for service with the Luftwaffe. After a protracted to-and-fro-ing he was accepted, with the official restriction on his service papers – 'without rank'. That he was permitted to fly again was certainly due to the influence of some leading Luftwaffe personalities, for whom anything the Nazi Party did was like a red rag to a bull.

We had hoped to acquire our combat training in Krakau, so that we could be transferred to an operational unit as quickly as possible, but this was just wishful thinking. Apart from the poor 'top' personnel, they had only a few older Do 17Es with BMW VI engines, usually unserviceable – which, considering the activity (or lack of it) there, did not surprise me in the least.

Yesterday I made my first flight at Krakau, accompanied by a Feldwebel named Seifert. He was a complete stranger to me, but we were both detailed to the same aircraft, on which I was to start my retraining on bombers.

We climb in, fasten our seat harnesses, and I await further developments. The flight mechanic is already in his place, all set to go. It was the first time I had set my foot inside a Do 17 and I was quite pleased about the aircraft. Because of its elegant shape, it had been nicknamed 'the Flying Pencil', and it was on a special DB 600-powered version of this type of aircraft that Polte* had won the speed contest at the Zürich Air show two years before the war. The machine looked nice and streamlined, but there was not much room in the 'office' for the three-man crew. On the other hand, the seating arrangements were so well thought-out that the crew members did not get in each other's way.

Being new on the type, I let the flight mechanic explain all the necessary handles and instruments: the undercarriage activating levers, landing flaps, engine-starting installation, the fuel cross-pumping system, and so on. As Seifert does not say a word, I ask him if we could start the engines and taxi away. 'Go ahead, as far as I am concerned!' he replies.

Together with the flight mechanic I start the engines – I already knew the BMW VI from the He 70 I had flown before – and let them warm up before running up to full power. So far, so good: the engines throttled back, the revs and temperatures in order, I taxi to the take-off runway over the snow-covered field. The weather is not exactly cheerful. The cloud base is only about 100 to 300 metres (300 to 1,000 ft) high, with occasional snow showers, and the visibility is limited to just 1,000 metres. Apart from mine, there is only one other aircraft flying at the time, and I can take off right away.

Seifert still does not utter a word, and so I set the flaps to take-off position, move the aircraft in the correct direction on the runway

* 4th International Military Aircraft Competition at Zürich-Dubendorf 23 July – 1 August 1937, when the unarmed Do 17M V1 prototype powered by two DB 6ol engines and flown by Maj Polte and Gen Milch were outright winners of the Alpine Round Flight – proving 40 km/h (25 mph) faster than the best contemporary French fighter, the Dewoitine D.510. The standard Do 17 bombers were heavier and had less powerful engines. Tr.

Peter Wilhelm Stahl during his flight training days in 1934. The aircraft is a Focke-Wulf FW 44 Stieglitz.

and receive the 'clear to take off' signal from the flight controller. I push the throttles forward, listen to the engines while having a quick glance at the instrument panel – the temperatures and revs seem to be right – and then let go of the brakes.

We take off surprisingly quickly and, although a complete newcomer on the type, I have the machine well in hand right away. After becoming airborne I signal to the flight mechanic to retract the undercarriage and then, as a matter of habit, throttle back both engines to climbing performance. I am just about feeling around behind my seat for the hand-wheel to retract the flaps when the flight mechanic suddenly starts giving me agitated signs, pointing at the port engine.

'The engine is on fire!' he then shouts in my ear. A quick glance shows thick yellow-white smoke billowing up from under the engine cowling and leaving a thick trail behind the aircraft and well away to the rear. We are just a few metres high and over the airfield perimeter. Ahead to the west the ground rises, dotted with the small houses of a settlement. Next moment the whole cabin is full of thick smoke and I lose all visual contact with the world outside. With some effort I find the blind flying instruments on the strange instrument panel, and try to hold the machine straight to gain some height to begin with! Willing the Do 17 to keep on climbing, I order the flight mechanic to switch off the fuel to the burning engine and simultaneously whip out its ignition key. With flying hands I search among the various levers for the one regulating the airscrew pitch, seeking to feather the propeller blades of the sick engine, and then stop it revolving altogether.

By now we have managed to reach an altitude of 50 metres and whizz along just over the roofs and trees! The burning engine begins to turn over more slowly, and finally stops completely, after some last jerks. Our cramped cabin is still full of acrid smoke, and I can just about make out the instruments. Due to the sideways pull of the starboard engine I have to exert a strong pressure on the opposite rudder pedal, and eventually have practically to stand on it. The necessary equalising pressure is so strong that my knee begins to tremble. But I must hold on! I have only one thought in mind: to gain altitude and speed – speed is a must to save our lives! And I know full well that the smallest error will inevitably end in a crash.

A pre-war Do 17E bomber, dubbed 'The Flying Pencil'. By 1940 all aircraft of this type had been relegated to Luftwaffe bomber training schools, and it was on a Do 17E that the author had some hair-raising experiences early in 1940.

The Do 17Z, a heavier and more powerful development of the 'Flying Pencil', was one of the operational aircraft used by Luftwaffe bomber training units to gain 'type flying' experience.

To think even further ahead, to be afraid, or lose my nerve – I just haven't got the time for all that!

At last on our one engine we do begin to gain some height, laboriously climbing higher metre by metre. While I am constantly prepared for the splintering crash of running into some obstacle or other, the acrid glycol smoke begins to clear in the cabin and I can see again. The first thing I notice is that the undercarriage is still not fully retracted. I already know that this procedure takes a bit of time on the Do 17, and with only one engine running it would naturally take twice as long. There is nothing I can do about that now.

By careful movements of the controls I then ascertain that the machine sits quite well in the air on only one engine, even just after becoming airborne, and with flaps still in take-off position. In fact all controls respond well, and give the right feel. I have gained confidence in the aircraft, but now and then for a moment I get into a real panic! But that only lasts for an instant – it's because I suddenly become frightened about the whole idiotic situation I am in, and for just that moment don't quite know what will happen next, and how I am going to get the big bird back on the ground again. But this panicky feeling is gone just as quickly as it grabbed me.

Somehow we have climbed to an altitude of about 100 m (330 ft) and the first cloud tatters whizz past the transparent panels of my cabin. I press forward lightly on the control column, and am pleased to note that the machine gains speed quite nicely without losing any appreciable height. The undercarriage too seems fully retracted by now – at least I cannot see anything of it when I briefly take my eyes off the instrument panel and hazard a quick glance outside. Things are looking better now, and I risk a careful move on the handwheel to retract the flaps. Steady, steady, because this reduces the lift, but the machine starts gaining more speed and now really flies. I throttle back the starboard engine to avoid overloading it, and then look around at my crew.

What a gang! The flight mechanic sits cowering behind my seat, chalk-white in face, and seems to have added up the pro's and con's, in preparation for the end of his life

The Feldwebel is excitedly manipulating the wireless set and calling out something to me. I cannot make out what he is trying to say, but he too is chalk-white in face and has an anxious look in his wide-open eyes. Then he crawls forward and shouts in my ear that he cannot get any contact with the ground station because the wireless set seems to be unserviceable, and what should he do now?

'Are you a wireless operator then?' I shout, and he nods his head vigorously and asserts once more that with the best will in the world he cannot do anything because of the dud set. Who cares!

'And I thought you were the pilot who was going to retrain me on this type!' No, he says, Leutnant Kraus had detailed him to be my wireless operator, and that is all he knew.

That's really good news! Nothing for it now, Mr Stahl, you will have to make the best of it on your own!

Where is the airfield? Above all, I must get back to the field, and see if I can get down on one engine. Fortunately, out of an old habit as a weather observation pilot, I had pressed my stopwatch on take-off, so at least I've an idea of the distance flown since becoming airborne. I turn a careful shallow blind-flying bank, keeping to the cloud base, until after a seemingly endless 'slither-skid' I am finally on a reciprocal course. I hold this exactly on the dot and fly off the seconds until the airfield should appear beneath us again. Of course, it is impossible to be quite accurate because I could not hold the machine on a straight flight path while climbing. The time is up, but down below we can see anything but our airfield! Visibility is very bad, and I can virtually see only whatever happens to be directly underneath. To make things even worse, it is snowing harder, and I have to revert to pure blind flying again! There is nothing for it now but a systematic search of the whole area. My only aids are the compass, the stopwatch, and my own eyes. If only I had at least got to know the area, or my two Charlies had been of some assistance in this search! But both of them are still just sitting there trembling, with wide-open childish eyes following my every move. No, it is up to me alone.

The Dornier flies on and I pass over railway tracks, street crossings, the town itself, the river, anything but the airfield. Fortunately the remaining BMW VI does its job well, and I find the machine a joy to fly on one engine.

After about half an hour of fruitless search I suddenly spot an aircraft on the ground in between the snow-clouds – the airfield! A quick squeeze on the stopwatch and a clean straight flight according to my watch and compass, followed by a 180 degree turn and an approach for landing. I let the undercarriage be lowered, and then slowly wind down the landing flaps myself. Very carefully I start losing height, expecting the field to appear before me at any moment. Having never landed this type before, I've no idea if I am too fast or too slow; it's pure guesswork now!

But it does not work out the first time; I miss the airfield by some 50 metres up and have to go around again. Keep calm, keep calm! Around again in the clouds, the big bird is as good-natured as an old cow, and I am right in line the second time around. I let the Dornier float, pull slowly on the control column, then press down, because I had flattened out a bit too high, down again, and then I pull the control column right back into my body, and reach for the throttle.

Even then, it nearly came to a crash, because in the instant I chopped the throttle, the hard-trimmed rudder suddenly swung the machine into a sideways- sliding movement I managed to correct with swift opposite rudder just before touching down. The wheels hiss through the deep snow, we are being slowed down softly, and come to a standstill in the middle of the airfield. I switch off the engine, take my foot off the rudder pedal and manage to express my feelings in just one word: 'Shit!'

Then we climb out, step into the snow and look around. My two crewmates now look confident again, and tell me everything I did was really first-rate, and that they too – each on his own of course – had thought that's what should have been done and at just that moment!

'Well, it was fortunate that you two were with me, otherwise who knows what would have happened!'

28 February 1940
Low-level flying exercises. To complete our Krakau 'training' (some training that was!) I am given the task of dropping concrete bombs on the practice ground, followed by flying on a set course at low level.

In the meantime we have crewed up – they let us have freedom to select for ourselves who is going to fly with whom on operations. As my navigator I've picked Feldwebel Digeser, a bright Swabian and like myself a reservist. He's already flown in a bomber formation so he can bring some experience along into our 'shop! However, I can't find a wireless operator or air gunners to join me. I'm told not to worry about this; I'll find these missing crew members when I join the unit.

Fair enough: I take off with Digeser and a flight mechanic, and we drop our concrete 'eggs' more or less accurately on the target in several passes. Then I go down in a steep swoop from our 2,000 m altitude, right into the Vistula valley. Digeser has the map on his knees and navigates.

This kind of flying, only a few yards off the ground, demands complete attention, but is terrific fun with the Dornier. The big twin-engined bird reacts wonderfully to the lightest control movements, and it is pure joy to feel this response. But the real fun is still to come. Within a few minutes Digeser is completely lost, and I have to continue on my own, relying on the compass and the watch. Whenever I ask him where we are, he moves his finger around somewhere over the map, always hoping that some prominent ground feature will appear to help him find his way again! That's the trouble: these fellows simply have too little practical flying experience. I never cease to wonder at how carefree and unconcerned they are when they climb into the aircraft! Just trust the pilot!

In the meantime this low-level flying is giving me no end of fun, and I could not care less where we are. Finding my way back home again does not bother me: it is a beautifully sunny winter's day, with endless visibility, made to order to enjoy some nice sporty flying for a change. I am one with the machine, listening to the comforting dampened tone of its engines and feeling the harmonious vibration of its metal body.

We fly over some miserable-looking Polish villages. Although the war has been over for some time, the peasants all seem to be scared of aircraft and fall flat on their faces in the snow, or run into their dilapidated houses when we whizz over them. I do feel sorry for the people, but I cannot avoid them at this speed and low altitude; we are not doing this deliberately. Hardly are they in my field of vision when we are over them and away again.

Now we arrive over an area where the signs of fighting are still visible: burned-down villages and blown-up bridges mark the way the beaten Polish army retreated. In between we can spot hurriedly-dug trenches and long-since vacated positions, with an abandoned field gun or burned-out vehicles here and there. And always those blown-up bridges over the river, one after another. Next we fly over a railway line where the work of German Stukas is still clearly evident: bomb-hits right in the centre of a railway station, and not far from it a complete train thrown off the embankment and now lying on its back alongside it. It's time we turned back.

2 March 1940

Today we are on our way! We take leave of Krakau: Eddy Digeser, Leo Krantz and myself – it is really nice that the three of us can remain together. We are posted to Ergänzungs-Kampfgruppe Ju 88 (Training and Replacement Bomber Group) at Greifswald. We are proud as anything at being the first ones chosen from the whole bunch, and cannot wait to get going. To be selected to fly the Ju 88 is really something – one hears all kinds of stories about this wonder bird. The Ju 88 is supposed to be so fast and agile that it can even hold its own in combat against enemy fighters, or so they say.

One final drive with the horse sleigh into the town, to take leave of the place, and just three hours later we are on the train to Berlin. It turns out to be a miserable night ride, arriving early in the morning. We have a short break there, and are then on our way again the same afternoon as per orders.

On arriving at Greifswald I meet Oberleutnant (Flying Officer) Meinhof again, another ex-Krakauer. We first met each other while detailed to carry out a rather nasty bad-weather flight from Krakau to Breslau and it was during this flight that we became closely acquainted despite the difference in our ranks.

3 March 1940

I have to move again, to the neighbouring Gruppe (Group) at Barth. The station commander, who knows all about the 'Leo Case', doesn't want to see another one in the secret in the same group as Leo. He is quite frank about this to me, and I can understand his reasons. However painful the parting seemed at first, now I am more pleased about this, because I've been seeing another side of Leo, his behaviour towards the fairer sex, which was not exactly up my street. Nevertheless, we had a really good farewell celebration.

CHAPTER TWO

The Ju 88

5 April 1940, Barth, Pomerania
I have been detailed to 1. Staffel and, as the only reservist there, I do not exactly have an easy life.

If I thought I would get my hands on a Ju 88 right away I was to be sadly disappointed. True, I have been recognised as an old hand and I participate in training flights with older types of plane only when it suits me, but that's all. The Ju 88 is something special, so completely different from anything known before that one is permitted to fly the aircraft only after the most thorough theoretical training on the ground.

To begin with, there is that very complicated hydraulic system, activating undercarriage, landing flaps, dive brakes, the automatic dive pull-out installation, and locking the tailwheel, with the duplicated manual emergency system worked by a hand pump. All that had to be learned, studied and understood. An innovation compared to previous modern aircraft types in the world is that the Ju 88 was designed as a possible one-man aircraft, meaning that although it has a crew of four (pilot, bomb aimer/navigator, wireless operator and gunner), if need be the pilot can carry out all the functions necessary during an operational flight from his own seat. In other words, he flies the aircraft, looks after both engines, controls and activates the fuel and oil cross-pumping system, handles all levers activating the hydraulics, and takes over the radio navigation as far as direction-finding from the aircraft is concerned. This was really something quite new.*

---

* It must have accounted for the safe return of many battle-scarred Ju 88s with injured crew members.

The entry into the cabin which accommodates the entire crew is by means of a folding ladder, part of the hinged ventral gun position known as 'Bola' (from *Bodenlafette*). Climbing up the ladder, one first stands near the ventral gun position itself (normally occupied by a prone gunner facing backwards when flying on operations.) Another step higher brings one level with the wireless operator's seat and, ahead of it, the pilot's and bomb aimer's seats. The wireless operator sits facing backwards, with all his equipment distributed around him close at hand. In addition to his main task he also serves two dorsal machine guns fitted separately in ball-type mounts with circular bullet-proof glass panels. Another task he has to fulfil during an operational flight is to look after the emergency fuel-pumping system, and a number of levers that activate the fuel cross-pumping installation to cope with engine failure or trouble with auxiliary fuel pumps. Finally, it is also up to the wireless operator to jettison the cabin roof in an emergency, either before an emrgency landing, or a bale-out by parachute.

The 70-metre long trailing aerial is released and retracted by means of an electric motor. And it mustn't be forgotten!

But the bomb aimer has other duties too, apart from assisting the pilot with navigation and looking after the bomb system's fuse-setting mechanism and release selector. During the flight he also observes the engine control instruments and, on instructions from the pilot, handles various switches (which are more conveniently situated for him) that activate the fuel cross-pumping system. As a rule he also carries out direction-finding from the aircraft and, in combat, has a machine gun which can also be fixed, to fire forward. In addition to all this, there is an auxiliary control column for the bomb aimer if the pilot becomes a casualty. To this end, the bomb-aimers are given a rudimentary training that would enable them to fly the aircraft long enough (all being reasonably well!) on their own, at least over their own territory, to give the other crew-members a chance to bale out. They have really thought of everything.

The design and layout of the pilot's position seems a truly ideal solution to me. Thanks to the fully glazed nose section of the fuselage visibility is unrestricted in all directions, even vertically downwards. All the necessary levers and instruments for take-off,

A Ju 88A-1 bomber in flight, showing the distinctive angled wing shape. Owing to the almost equal length of both engine nacelles and the fuselage ahead of the wing, the Ju 88A was generally described by German aircraft recognition services as the 'Three-finger Ju' to differentiate it from the superficially similar Bristol Blenheim during the early stages of hostilities. Despite these and other obvious recognition points errors were common, sometimes with tragic results.

Early production Ju 88A-1 bombers formed the initial equipment of KG 30, the first Luftwaffe unit to operate this new aircraft.

flight, power plant control, fuel and oil systems, navigation and combat are clearly arranged and within easy reach. Sitting there, one feels like an organ player with this array of various keys and knobs at one's hands and feet. The left hand alone has to look after a whole series of seemingly confusing levers, buttons and switches fitted all along the side 'control table' as far as one can reach forwards and backwards from the seat. However, one experiences a feeling of initial confusion in every strange aircraft type before the functions of all the levers, knobs and switches are learned and memorised. In the Ju 88 the task is made easier by the different shapes of the various handles, quickly identifiable by feel alone as the 'right' ones – so important in darkness and in the heat of battle, looking outward all the time.

On the other hand, the instrument panel shows hardly any innovations compared to other multi-engined aircraft. The flight and power-plant instruments, and the fuel capacity gauges are all concentrated in sensible groups: I can take in the required information at a glance. Apart from that, this layout allows the instrument panel itself to be much smaller and narrower, presenting much less obstruction to the pilot's field of vision.

Here at Barth we will be trained by Junkers factory engineers from morning till night for six weeks to learn every detail of the airframe and Jumo engines. Since I've had more to do with the Ju 88, I am no longer disappointed at failing to become a fighter pilot. Quite the opposite: I have realised now how much more fascinating the work of a bomber pilot from the flying and technical points of view is.

Anyway, the emphasis in operational tactics with the Ju 88 is on diving attacks, in other words on individual attacks on point targets – in this respect very similar to fighter attacks.

Our days in Barth are fully taken up with intensive theoretical instruction in the lecture halls, and what is known as 'type flying', gaining flying experience on different types of single- and multi-engined aircraft. These include various versions of the Do 17, He 111, Ju 87, Ju 52, and a number of smaller 'birds' – but still no Ju 88 as yet!

On the Ju 87 we get acquainted with dive bombing tactics. I find it really enjoyable to tip this truly good-natured kite on its head at about 3-4,000 metres altitude, and then go down in a vertical dive, aiming for the imaginary target like a hawk.

Clumsy and awkward as the Ju 87 may look – its nickname is 'Jolanthe'!* – it's very good-tempered to fly. All of us like the Ju 87 a lot, and some even fly aerobatics with it. Pity that its flight endurance is only two and half hours! Whatever the plane, I most certainly prefer being up there to the seemingly interminable instruction on the ground, although I fully realise how important it is for us all.

15 April 1940

We are now so full of lecture-room knowledge of all kinds that we are fed up to the teeth with it, and are fervently wishing it to end, so we can finally start retraining on the Ju 88. But unfortunately we are not there yet!

Today I had a change of routine: I am instructed to proceed to Ansbach to collect a Do 17Z and fly it back here. I am on my way in no time!

One of the things that I notice in Ansbach is that one can still get sausages in a Bavarian *Gasthaus* without meat coupons; I have to keep that in mind!

On the airfield I have an unexpected meeting with Egon Waldmann who is in charge of the technical management. This is a really pleasant surprise! As airmen we shared quite a few experiences in 1934-1936, and I recall particularly a flight in a storm from Dornstadt to Würzburg and back, with two Heinkel He 72 Kadett biplanes.

We arrived at the Schwabisch Alb in really thick weather and crept behind each other, hedge-hopping and practically rolling along the footpaths through the countryside. Near Bopfingen, in very thick cloud and gusty weather, we just had to give up our cross-country jaunt. We agreed with each other by sign-language that we would have to make an emergency landing somewhere to be on the safe side. We started looking around for a suitable patch, but the weather was so bad that it seemed a hopeless task. Every time a

---

* A name given to the *Glücksschwein*, the lucky pig, a traditional German symbol of good fortune. Used as a unit symbol by the first three Ju 87A Stukas tested in Spain in autumn 1937. (Tr.)

The Geschwaderstab flight of KG 30 in combat formation, with 'Nordpol-Anton' nearest.

likely-looking field loomed towards us through the fog it was already too late to chop the throttle and land. It had to be done in one go – with a small sports aircraft like the He 72 it was impossible to make a second approach in accordance with blind-flying rules. I thought it was best to split up and continue looking separately, and took my leave from Egon again in sign language – or so I thought. Once on my own, I managed to find my way to Ansbach airfield, but when I levelled off to land suddenly there was Egon in his Kadett right behind me, also coming in to land! On the ground, he told me that he had completely lost his way and was really glad when I had taken the lead. That explained it: apparently his manual signals to me in the fog were intended to convey the message that he was lost, and did I know the way – not that he had decided to make an emergency landing on his own!

Over several good brandies we reminisced until late in the evening. Egon belonged to that class of airmen who could give up and forget everything for the sake of flying, and for that reason he was especially dear to me.

18 April 1940
Our kite is finally cleared for flight and I can start making my way back to Barth. The Do 17Z is another new type to me and I had hoped I would at least have one familiarisation flight with an experienced pilot before taking it up on my own. But it was not to be: they could not find anybody who had flown this type of aircraft before.

My only companion aboard is Aircraft Inspector Mohr who had accompanied me from Barth. Well, Mr Stahl, here we go again! Running up the engines and taxiing is no problem, but the take-off nearly ends in disaster. On this particular type the throttle levers had an arrestor catch that had to be released by lifting special buttons, to get full take-off power from the engines. This of course I did not know, and so I blithely push both 'gas hammers' forward till they ram home and let the big Dornier run free. True enough, I am a bit puzzled why the machine seems so lazy about picking up speed, but do not think much of it, because the habits of this particular buck are still strange to me.

The runway at Ansbach is not exactly long, but when one has to take off with only half power, it is definitely too short!

Anyway, I'm rolling along towards the airfield perimeter with its high fence, determined to become airborne. The big Dornier stumbles along like a lame duck from one patch of uneven ground to another and does not seem to care a hoot what I intend to do with it. In my mind I can already hear the crash. What's the matter with this thing? A short distance from the fence I push the control column briefly forward instead of pulling it towards me, giving the machine more or less free rein. It was really an act of desperation, but it helps the Dornier to draw its breath a bit, gain some speed and, lo and behold, we are airborne!

To be sure, the kite sinks down again just the other side of the fence, right in the direction of a freshly-ploughed field, but the wheels do not touch the ground, and slowly, ever so slowly, we gain height, inch by inch. It is fortunate that the undercarriage can be retracted relatively quickly. This helps to reduce drag, because right ahead of us is a village and I doubt it very much if I can get over the roofs of its houses with my wheels still down! Helped along by a feeble turn – I could not even call it a flat curve – I slide past the church steeple, and then I am really pleased to note that we are now some 20 metres off the ground! The speed too has built up in the meantime, so that we are more or less in flying condition. On reaching decent altitude I turn back to the airfield and circle it several times, before preparing to land with trembling knees.

Taking great care I first distance myself from the field, drop the undercarriage, set the landing flaps, throttle back both engines a bit and then try out how the big Dornier behaves in this condition. After that I let it float down towards the landing cross, still with trembling knees. The fence whizzes past just under our belly, I pull the throttle lever back and hold the machine level, the wheels touch the ground ever so softly and the big Dornier nicely rolls to a stop as if nothing had happened. I take a deep breath and, if I ever had a load on my mind, it drops off now!

On leaving the machine, Mohr, who had sat next to me through this hair-raising ordeal with a self-important inspector's face, simply comments that this is obviously a fine aircraft that lets itself be flown easily. He is really an angel, but a truly ingenuous one! Of course, all that matters to him is that the aircraft is on hand as requested, that it flies all right, and that the papers are in order. And so they were, and we could make our way back to Barth – or could we?

At the airfield weather office they now tried to advise me against flying because clouds were building up in the Mittelgebirge mountain range area and we could not cross them without flying blind. But I had no wireless operator, and therefore was not permitted to fly blind – 'It says so here in the rules!' Of course I knew that too, but was determined to get back home, and started haggling with the weather station people and flight control. It took some time, but I was finally given permission to fly back to Barth in a round-about route via Silesia and Frankfurt/Oder.

Which pilot does not know of this haggling with the airfield authorities to get permission to fly in uncertain weather conditions? The whole thing is so obvious to me: when preparing his forecasts the weather man plays safe and gives the expected route weather a forecast worse than the real one because he would be held responsible if anything went wrong. Then there is the flight controller who takes his weather man's forecast and adds a safety factor on his own part. Taken together, the weather forecasts for cross-country flights in such conditions are often far worse than the weather really is. So many flights that could have been accomplished without undue difficulty never take place, because the pilots have been advised against flying by such people – unfortunately almost exclusively non-airmen.

My hint that after all I possessed blind-flying instructor's qualifications, and had quite a bit of experience from my days as a weather observation pilot before the war, fell on deaf ears, on account of my low service rank, that was obvious. Nevertheless, after protracted negotiations – in the end even marshalling the help of my good friend Egon Waldmann, who spoke up on my behalf, I finally managed to obtain the necessary permission to take off, with the proviso that I would fly around that 'bad' area.

To be on the safe side, I waited until the next weather report came through, in the meantime requesting my machine tanked up to full capacity to have some reserve fuel; and then had a meal at Egon's invitation. But instead of improving, the weather got worse, and if I did not want to risk complete grounding I had to get away as quickly as possible. After I'd rechecked everything twice, it was 1505 hrs when I pushed the throttles forward – this time right to the hilt – and rumbled away with a machine under my behind that behaved the way it should at take-off, and with a companion next to me who was not exactly overjoyed, in expectation of a possible bad weather flight.

To begin with I fly directly towards the Thüringer Forest, hoping somehow to sneak through there, but am forced to realise pretty soon that it is impossible. The weather has become stinking bad already in the area west of Bamberg, and this time I really have to give the weather frog* at Ansbach his due: he was right. I then bank towards the east, following the course I had already marked in red on my map, and prepare myself for a battle against atmospheric difficulties. And so it came to pass, as they say.

In parts, the clouds are almost down to the ground level, while occasionally visibility is surprisingly good so that I can relax a bit after literally hopping over fences and church steeples. I keep near the southern edge of the Thüringer Forest and the Fichtel mountain range in the hope of finding some escape northwards. The beautiful Franconian countryside glides past me only 1,000ft or so underneath because in this area I'm forced so close to the ground. It is at times like these, when the machine is whizzing ahead at high speed that one regrets as a pilot not being able to stop and stand still when something really nice flits past underneath. We fly over a small locality: the dear old houses look as if they are scattered around in the narrow valley by a child's playful hand. Despite the bad weather – the clouds both sides of us hang down to the mountain ridges – I just cannot fly past this place without pulling a steep bank to have at least a few quick glances at the scene below. It seems that time has stood still here for hundreds of years.

After getting back on course I search on the map and find that this little place is called Berneck. I like it so much that I make up my mind that I will spend my first holidays there with *her*, when this war is over!

But the weather gives me no more time for such wishful thinking, and soon becomes very uncomfortable. Tattered bits of cloud shoot

* *Wetterfrösche* = weather frogs: Luftwaffe slang for their meteorological personnel. Probably because German (and French) mythology has it that the frog is a weather expert! (Tr.)

past my glass-house and, just as I pull the machine a bit higher when the clouds overhead and around seem to be getting brighter, everything turns black and dark, and I have to go down again! In a situation like this one is not very happy about getting too far from the ground, and apart from that, I am forbidden to fly blind without a wireless operator. In the end the whole business becomes too awkward and too dangerous for me, and I have to make up my mind either to turn back or continue flying blind. To turn back – never! Somehow and somewhere I am bound to come out of this murk and catch sight of the ground again. A slight backward movement of the control column, and the earth beneath us starts to recede and the fields and forests grow hazy in the grey fog. My eyes and senses are now concentrating on the instruments. A quick glance around and below outside: nothing but endless cloud! The earth is already so far away beneath us that no trace of it can be seen, and I am all alone with my instruments. My eyes are glued to the various dials and figures: the turn-and-bank indicator, compass, variometer, Sperry artificial horizon, and the sensitive altimeter. My whole body now lives only with the aircraft: I have to 'switch off' and forget all about flying by feel as a pilot and rely on sheer common sense, trusting the scientific instruments.

The Dornier climbs steadily. Ahead of us is the Mittelgebirge mountain range which in this area is nearly 1,000 metres high, but the empty machine gains height at a good rate and I have soon reached the necessary safety altitude. At this point I could just fly straight ahead, but I have the impression that the clouds are becoming lighter overhead, and I keep on climbing in the hope of getting through at the top. The temperature is sinking constantly, and soon it is near zero. Without taking my eyes off instruments I call out to my companion to look for any signs of ice so that I can react at once, either by interrupting my climb to find another level with more tolerable temperature, or by climbing through the critical zone as quickly as possible. But Mohr remains silent, and it is up to me alone.

The Dornier continues climbing bravely and then it becomes obvious that the sunlight will soon break through; the thick murk pulls past the cabin in more and more uneven swathes, then there are only tattered bits of clouds, and suddenly the sunshine reflects off the instrument panel. We are through!

I can breathe easily again and take my eyes off the instruments, to enjoy that ever-fascinating image when an aircraft surfaces out of the clouds into the radiant lightness and endless solitude of the cloud scenery. At this time the eyes see only two colours, the saturated, indescribably beautiful blue of the sky that fades only a shade towards the horizon, and the blinding whiteness of the clouds. On these occasions I am always ever more impressed by the limitless extent and solitude one leaps into so suddenly, an experience that is overwhelming even though it has become more or less a daily event.

My good companion Mohr, apparently living in fear, is nothing but a nuisance now. He has suddenly become more active and shouts something in my ear and actually laughs, but I have no idea what he is on about.

The shadow of my machine speeds over the white cotton wool sea underneath, and is framed by a circular rainbow that at times grows smaller or enormously wide according to the rhythm of the wavy cloud surface.

I take the map on my knees and catch up on my navigation: if the wind forecasts were right, I have to fly a course of 356 degrees, then I would get past Berlin just west of it and come out somewhere in the Barth area after an estimated flight-time of 1 hr 25 mins. Of course, this calculation cannot lay any claims to accuracy, because I do not know my exact present position, but breaking through cloud cover near the coastal area is not so much of a problem because there are no mountains or other obstacles. That being so, I can give myself up completely to the joy of flying.

I believe that airmen love nothing more than solitude, the special sky-loneliness that is beyond all measure and perception of people outside our profession, who probably could not understand or even conceive what we meet between the sky and the earth, and the clouds and the sun.

I loosen my harness belts and make myself as comfortable as possible in the seat. Then I pull the Neophan* glasses over my eyes and let the machine skim ahead just over the cloud surface. This kind of flying is sheer joy! Now I only have to keep an eye on the

---

* Trade name of standard Luftwaffe sunglasses. (Tr)

direction-indicator of my distant-reading compass to correct any deviation from the flight path. I do not have to bother about any other navigational problems because without a wireless operator I have no chance of solving them anyway!

Somewhere in the Magdeburg-Berlin area the white blanket beneath us opens up a bit, and deep down there I can distinguish seemingly dark, almost black fields, lighter highways, a railway track and smaller inhabited places, before the clouds close in again. However, these few fleeting details are insufficient for proper ground orientation, although they offer the hope that these gaps in the cloud cover will increase in size and I can soon find my way down again.

Just as I am about to fasten my harness again Mohr suddenly nudges me in the ribs and excitedly points downwards on the right. Alarmed, I whip the Dornier around in a tight turn because I have no idea what he is pointing at, and then through a large hole in the clouds I spot an airfield with wetly-shining hangar roofs and concreted runways – it seems to be raining down there. And then I recognise the airfield: it is Rechlin, near Lake Müritz. This means I am exactly on course and can cut through the clouds in the direction of my destination without any more worry.

I straighten out the machine back on the flight path, and throttle back the engines a bit to start losing altitude. Immediately we are back in the clouds again and everything quickly becomes darker all around. I push the sunglasses back on my forehead, and my eyes are once again glued to the instruments. With the elevators, I hold the sinking speed to 4 metres per second and we are through into the clear sky already! – at 800 metres altitude, after having had several brief glimpses of the ground.

In the area north of Berlin to the shores of the Baltic Sea I can find my way without any maps, and we are soon near Barth.

Over the base I fly a regulation turn in accordance with my service position and rank, carry out the procedures necessary for a landing, float in, touch down near the landing cross and taxi over to my parking area.

When I have switched off the engines and the propellers have made their last rotations to come to a full stop accompanied by the clatter of cylinder valves, the sudden silence is so brutal that I am instantly wide awake. During those 2 hours and 45 minutes the flight had lasted I had become a 'civilian' again. Now I am back on the ground as Unteroffizier Stahl. The point is driven home when, after leaving the aircraft, I first happen to run into an Oberfeldwebel who is always mad at me because, first, I receive the special flying provisions, second, I am a reservist, third, I am quite undeservedly piloting an aircraft which he has to look after, and fourth, because of higher rank he can be mad at me when he feels like it.

After this reintroduction to military procedure I have to report at the airfield flying control office to check in my flight log book. There, behind a suitably impressive desk, will sit a Hauptmann (captain) who has at long last, (and only just!) been promoted to that rank.

This Hauptmann is not interested in what experiences I have gone through during the past two and three quarter hours. Instead, he will cast his critical eye over the fit of my uniform, and probably snarl at me because my salute on entering his office was not quite up to regulation standard, and then devote his attention to searching my flight log book and other documents for things that do not correspond to regulations! Fortunately he has no idea of flying, despite occupying the post of Air Traffic Officer. I have already learned the procedure, and snap to attention accordingly here, make my report there, and after many 'yes, sirs', finally arrive at Staffel headquarters, where I report back from my delivery flight ('without any special events') to Oberleutnant Alisch.

Here in a flying unit I meet a completely different tone. – 'Well, what was it like?' – 'Did you manage to get the kite down all right?' – 'What's doing at Ansbach?' – 'Didn't get up to any mischief on the way, did you?' – these are the kind of questions that one meets on arrival, friendly greetings without any special emphasis on authority or difference in rank.

These are the things that always reconcile me to uniform: there are no *Bettenbauer** in a bunch of real airmen.

25 April 1940
Today I learned about something new in military flying – at least

---

* Literally 'bed-maker', German military slang for a stickler for regulations. (Tr.)

something new for me as a professional airman: a crash. A crash is what a person in civvy street would describe as an accident. In our flying business there are the ordinary crashes and the 'giant Californian crashes', as they used to be called.

In an ordinary crash only a few bits and pieces fly through the air, there is less damage to man and machine, and therefore less paperwork. Apart from that, the expected penalties, if it was the pilot's fault, are also lighter.

A 'giant Californian crash' on the other hand leaves behind a lot of splintered and twisted stuff, and usually a lot more blood is lost. The other factors, such as paperwork, penalties, damage to crops and so on, are correspondingly heavier. Most crashes are the result of carelessness, or bravado, more rarely ineptitude, and really very seldom because of technical faults.

I have often thought about why so many aircraft and people are killed in military flying. It could not be because of instruction or training, nor is it because of the technical conditon of the material in use. Both the training and the state of machines are first rate, and the personnel on the job are likewise good.

The problem is a psychological one and is to be found in the selection and subsequent guidance of the flying personnel.

My old flying instructor Huppenbauer, known as 'Huppes', told us 'young hares' once in spring 1934: 'You have come to me to learn flying. You have been selected from many, and a dozen doctors have tapped and examined you. But don't flatter yourselves because of that: There are a lot of healthy, sane blockheads around too.'

In my opinion, he had hit the nail squarely on the head. The selection of flying personnel should not be made dependent on the judgment of doctors but first and foremost attention should be paid to the opinions of experienced airmen and flying instructors. Unfortunately this hardly ever took place and when it finally did, after the first major errors, then it was usually too late: the unsuitable 'healthy blockhead' was already established in his career, and there was no easy way to squeeze him out of it again. Lack of technical understanding, plus bureaucracy, in military institutions are things against which the healthy airman's common sense is simply powerless.

Hardly a day goes by here at Barth without some kind of crash, and it is often surprising that the participants get away without serious injury. But today things took a turn for worse, and something ghastly happened.

According to our training schedule, it was to be night flying with Do 17Zs and two aircraft were in the air, keeping a uniform distance from each other. While turning my prescribed circuits around the airfield I kept a careful eye on the other machine to avoid any mutual interference. I was just about to come in to land again when underneath me I noticed the navigation lights of another aircraft speeding along the runway for a take-off. And then it happened. I was concentrating on my landing procedure when suddenly the other machine pulled past in front of me like a flaming torch! I immediately rammed the throttles forward to go around again, flying at first directly behind the fiery trail that was growing visibly bigger. At the speed and direction I was flying I became a helpless witness to the tragedy. The pilot of this aircraft was obviously trying to attempt a belly landing to save the lives of his crew, and went into a flat turn, but he was unsuccessful. The fiery crash happened right underneath me, and I will never forget that horrible sight. The flames spread out in all directions, leaving a great bright red patch in the middle of the night – their funeral pyre. The realisation that it was only by pure chance that I was not piloting the doomed machine left me chilled with fright, and I made my last landing approach with trembling knees.

According to regulations I reported what I had observed of the crash, but it was only a formality: the entire crew had been killed.

There followed the usual investigation, but it was impossible to establish the cause of this accident. Perhaps the pilot had made a gross error of judgment: why didn't he continue flying straight ahead and attempt a belly-landing on the airfield instead of turning away to come down in the open countryside? According to all experience, even a burning aircraft would still remain controllable for a relatively long time, and the pilot should have known that a landing outside the airfield on a pitch black night could only have a fatal outcome. All this points to human failure as a cause of this fatal crash, although the possibility of a technical fault could not be entirely ruled out.

In addition to extensive experience gained in flying training, a real pilot should also possess certain exceptional characteristics: intelligence, a cool head, quick reactions, a feel for technical coherence, and an exact knowledge of 'his' element – the wind, weather and cloud formations. These points should be the criteria when selecting future airmen, and not such finicky points as whether a candidate should have more than four filled teeth or sweaty feet – not to mention the poor fellow with spectacles. Additional decisive criteria are the qualities of personal character and the way of life. These points were completely ignored in selection, and it would seem certain that here were hidden the reasons for many subsequent failures.

30 April 1940
Today is the 'big day': I fly the Junkers Ju 88 for the first time. My practical acquaintance with the machine is enhanced by Junkers test pilot Barnickel, and there is none of that instruction flight procedure here: I have to sit in the pilot's seat on my very first flight.

My first impressions are of the considerable difference in handling between this aircraft and all the other types I have flown before. For instance, the rudder is much less effective at low speeds, and demands increased attention from the pilot, especially at take-off and during landing approach. Generally speaking, this new Junkers bird is almost like a temperamental star or Diva: the Ju 88 seems to know that it is beautiful and interesting, and behaves accordingly. It is capable of suddenly doing quite surprising things without the slightest warning. These caprices are especially noticeable at take-off: one can hold the Ju 88 with the rudder nice and straight until the tail lifts off the ground. This movement does not seem to be to the Diva's liking, and the machine might make a sudden swing to port, which must be corrected with the opposite rudder at once, or else! The pilot really has to be on his toes and react immediately. The landing has to be carried out at an approach speed of 250 km/h (155 mph), levelling off at 215 km/h (134 mph). Here too the speed zone is relatively narrow and one has to keep closely within it at all times to avoid trouble.

However, I felt at home with the Diva right away and was permitted to fly the Ju 88 solo – with only a flight mechanic aboard – after only three training circuits. The thorough, hard theoretical instruction had paid off.

Unfortunately this is still not recognised by many budding pilots, who cheerfully absent themselves from 'classroom lessons' in the hope that things will turn out all right in the end, with the inevitable results.

Early May 1940

Suddenly everything is happening very quickly at Barth. Those pilots who had qualified on the Ju 88 now have to undergo a very intensive flight training programme, and we are longer in the air than on the ground. Trial dives, cross-country flights and bombing training flights follow each other without a break. But everything goes smoothly, and there are no hold-ups. One might well ask: why is this part of the training so successful?

Clearly because none of these activities had to be carried out according to military rules and regulations fixed in some distant staff office by people who had no practical knowledge of the realities. We on the other hand were guided by sober engineers who knew their aircraft like the backs of their own hands, and who helped us to get to know the new machine in a sensible way. From experience one could say that military regulations were prepared by people to whom this flying and engineering task seemed of only secondary importance.

CHAPTER THREE

Operational Unit

10 May 1940[*]

We have been discharged as fully trained Ju 88 pilots, and transferred to the only existing operational Ju 88 formation Kampfgeschwader 30 (KG 30). My orders were to report to II. Gruppe (Group) at Oldenburg.

I arrived with my crew as completed at Barth: Unteroffizier Gross, my bomb aimer and the man who would help me with navigation and be responsible for bomb release gear; Unteroffizier Harras, my radio operator; and Gefreiter (Lance Corporal) Arndt, my gunner.

And so I finally made it to an operational unit! For a while I had lost all hope of it, after they had told me at Barth that I should stay there as an instructor. But it had happened. We arrive here at Oldenburg around midday, and I have never yet seen such hectic activity on an airfield: since last night the unit has been in action against Holland. Ju 88s with the diving eagle insignia of KG 30 on their noses are taking off and landing all the time; at the command post crews are coming and going, dressed in oil-spattered flying suits, wearing life-jackets and fur-lined flying boots, and with yellow coverlets over their flying helmets. I catch bits of their conversation: '... any amount of fighters in the air!' ... '... dived on a ship in harbour ...' '... a convoy in the Channel ...' '... Rotterdam is aflame ...'

An Unteroffizier reports with a smile on his face that he has had 70 hits in his kite, which however did not prevent him from carrying out his operational task.

One Ju 88 taxies directly towards the command post where I am

---

[*] The day Germany invaded Holland, Belgium and Luxembourg.

standing: I feel almost like a war reporter or a representative of the Red Cross witnessing the scene that unfolds before my eyes. The entry hatch opens and I see a bloodied hand groping around underneath. Ground crew men run up to the machine and carefully pull out the badly wounded gunner from the ventral gondola. He is hit in the neck, and collapses on the field. An ambulance is on hand right away, and the casualty is whisked away to the hospital. More movement around the machine, and they carry out the bomb aimer/navigator – dead. It seems almost like a war film but this is stark reality, my first experience of war as it is.

While this is going on, there is no interruption in the activity on the airfield – take-off follows take-off, landing follows landing.

An open car drives past me and I look at the laughing faces of another Ju 88 crew. Hey, that's Leo Krantz with his men! What a coincidence that I should meet him here again! We exchange a few shouted words: Leo has already completed his third operational flight, and must be off again shortly. We have to leave everything till later.

11 May 1940
I have been detailed to 5.Staffel. I tried my best to join Leo in 1. Staffel but did not succeed. Apparently 5.Staffel has had heavy losses during the last few days: two Staffelkapitäne (squadron commanders) and three crews are missing, and they need replacements more than others.

14 May 1940
If I had thought I would be flying on operations right away, I was once again sadly disappointed.

When I report as one of the newcomers to Oberleutnant Schneider, our Staffelkapitän, he tells me he is pleased to have me in his Staffel, but I must understand that for the time being I have first to prove to their satisfaction that I can fly. Unfortunately there will be no time to check me out during a major operation like this and, apart from that, all available aircraft are needed for operational use. In the meantime I should settle in and wait until things have quietened down a bit before I can continue my training for operational service. It will be only then that a decision can be made if I am 'suitable' for KG 30.

With some years of experience behind me I am quite convinced that I can fly better than most of the crews at Oldenburg, but Schneider just will not have it. A real dry old stick!

16 May 1940

Holland is finished for our Geschwader, and the unit moves back to Perleberg, the home base of our Gruppe. I have the honour of ferrying a worn-out and only conditionally airworthy Ju 88.

17 May 1940, Perleberg

It is now clear that our Gruppe has had heavy losses during the recent operational period, and we are being reformed anew. A number of the crews are shunted about, and I am transferred from 5. to 4.Staffel, under Hauptmann Haas.

We are training again – intensively, hard and consistently. The ruled spaces in my flight log book are filling in: local flights, special flights to learn how to cope with various emergency situations in the air, cross-country flights, and mock dive-bombing attacks – again and again.

18 May 1940

It is a real joy to dive with the Ju 88. While the single-engined Ju 87 has a tendency to oscillate in a dive, especially just after winging over, and has to be held onto the target, the Ju 88 is rock-steady immediately after commencing a dive. To correct the diving angle one usually needs only a few minor adjustments of the trimming wheels positioned on the port cabin wall. There's sufficient time during a dive to observe what's going on, and look after the condition of the aircraft and the power plants. The warning signal to release the bombs is a hooter activated by an adjustable contact connected to the barometric altimeter.

My feeling of trust in this magnificent aircraft increases from day to day and hardens into real self-confidence.

Unfortunately this feeling also conceals within itself the danger of over-confidence: one gets carried away. During a practice dive without dive brakes speeding down at about 680 km/h (423 mph), I only just managed to pull out before touching the ground. I had to pull on the control column with all the strength I could muster to level off and to keep flying horizontally, only a few metres from the ground. This was a lesson I never forgot.

It was obvious that when diving a Ju 88 caution was a necessity; one could never be perfect. As a pilot one must rigidly respect all recognised or fixed limits. Otherwise these points would be rammed home by hard experience – or, as we used to say, one had to run down his own shoesoles until they clicked. And then, it was only the fortunate ones who got away with it unscathed while learning it the hard way. All I wanted was to put my practice bombs down even more accurately on the target and give the imaginary enemy even less opportunity to get the better of me. Yes, one *could* get carried away, with dire results.

27 May 1940

Anklam. Conclusion of our dive bombing training with practice dives on the target ship *Hessen** in the Baltic Sea off Dievenow. Very interesting, but not at all easy!

28 May 1940

Back to Perleberg. In the evening the whole Staffel drives out to Lake Langen near Lenzen, where everything was ready for a real feast. The prelude to this is an exercise with dinghies on what would happen in an emergency.

Just like that, the fully dressed aircrews are thrown into the water, and then have to make practical use of their emergency equipment according to previous training: blow up their life vests, prepare and board the dinghies, and finally row them ashore. The whole exercise is carried out like a sports competition, and I and my crew are the first to complete it.

The evening and the night are mild, and a large open logfire provides additional warmth and a romantic atmosphere. Everybody's in high spirits, we sing a lot, and there is enough to drink, but nobody overdoes it.

---

* A former pre-World War I battleship, 13,200 tons, one of the obsolete vessels Germany was allowed to keep under the terms of the Versailles Treaty. She was rebuilt as a remotely-controlled target ship in 1936-37; handed over to the Soviets in 1946. (Tr.)

Tonight I experience something new, a feeling of togetherness with these men: we are all mutually bound by flying and fate, and an uncertain future.

In the night we hear the news that Belgium too has capitulated today, and our forces are advancing further westwards. Will we still get there in time?

15 June 1940

We've received our transfer orders to Belgium. We are going to fly on operations after another two weeks of hard training. I feel in top form myself, although I am the only 'youngster' among the aircrews. I am detailed to 5.Staffel again.

We stand in groups in front of the big hangar, waiting for our take-off orders. Our destination is an advanced airfield near Louvain, close to a place called Le Coulot. It's surprising to someone who has not faced the enemy yet that although we all have had enough hard training in Germany, and want to be flying operationally, I cannot detect any enthusiasm in the faces of the men. I am not quite certain about my own feelings either. Somehow I had imagined this moment quite differently. Now there is like an emptiness inside me, and I feel lost among all these operationally experienced men. Perhaps I am simply afraid.

The others of course know that I'll shortly be making my first operational flight and give me all kinds of advice. I am most grateful for their concern, although I must have heard the stories a hundred times before. Perhaps my comrades also want to calm themselves, repeating how things worked out fine on this or that occasion.

It is now clear that I have been accepted in the 'club' and that the resentment felt against me as a 'reservist' is brushed away for good. Even Feldwebel Lorbeer is a changed person now, addressing me with the familiar '*Du*'. Before, he never missed an opportunity to point out that I was only a pitiful civilian and should not have any conceited notions about my flying ability.

My take-off orders arrive at 0930 hrs and I fly in a closed *Kette* (flight) with Feldwebeln Lorbeer and Friedrich. We are following another fifteen machines which have taken off before us. Feldwebel Lorbeer is an excellent leader, well aware that another two aircraft are flying echeloned left and right behind him, and we are keeping a tight formation. Our aircraft are soon in the clouds on the way upwards, and the climb continues to rise above them. We retain our tight formation in the clouds, even when the leading aircraft ahead of me is only just visible as a blurred shadow, and I cannot see anything of my wingman. When we are finally in the sun above the clouds we spot the other Ju 88s far ahead to the right. Keeping our tight formation, we are slowly gaining on them, when I notice one Ju 88 that has somehow lost its way and soon attaches itself to me. That pilot's so notorious for rotten formation flying that I am scared stiff: he is said to be the greatest *Uhrmacher** of the whole Gruppe. And now he's messing about so criminally on my starboard side that I am forced to leave our tight formation and fly independently. Just my luck!

We near the forward field and the formation heads down. We split up for landing. I am soon wrapped in clouds again but keep on downwards, catching my first sight of the ground only at 80 metres altitude.

After a prolonged search I at last find the advanced airfield, which consists of nothing more than just one large harvested field. I land from a tight turn and soon find out that I'm the first one down. The others land separately at longer intervals, while the dolt does not make it until one hour later.

The command post is situated at the edge of this field, and everything is very provisional. They have a proper field kitchen serving coffee, soup and roast chicken, although we have little time to enjoy this little luxury. The commanding officer opens the proceedings by telling us that we will be flying an operational sortie today. Exactly who, and how many aircraft, was not yet certain, but we all had to be ready just in case. The aircraft would carry a bomb load of just two 500 kg (1,102 lb) bombs, because the provisional airfield would not stand a heavier loading.

The awaited operational orders arrive by radio at 1500 hrs: seven Ju 88s have to attack the port of Cherbourg in the evening. This force will be led by Hauptmann Peters, and our Staffel is participating with Feldwebeln Kühnast, Lorbeer and Erkens and

---

* *Uhrmacher* (lit. clockmaker): derogatory Luftwaffe slang term for an airman who who keeps repeating the same errors; a dolt. (Tr.)

Unteroffizier Stahl. So this will be my combat début!

There follows a briefing, detailing the targets for individual crews. My task is to dive-bomb the warehouses in the port area. We take off with half-full tanks at 1630 hrs and fly to Amiens where there is a proper airfield and we can tank up for the long flight to our target. With full fuel tanks we would have never got off the ground from our advanced field. Even so, our take-off with the heavy machines from the provisionally levelled-off harvest field is dreadful, almost perilous. For an airman, the war does not begin when he comes face to face with the enemy!

All around the airfield at Amiens we still find traces of our British 'colleagues' who had operated from there just a short while ago. Jupp Harras, who always has a nose for such things, even manages to make his first war booty, in the shape of a large box of English sweets.

Hauptmann Peters takes off from the dusty runway at 1900 hrs on the dot, followed by myself. I have to chase blind through the thick clouds of dust left behind by my predecessor, and I am pleased when I finally feel my heavy machine leaving the ground. Mechanically I make the necessary movements, retracting the undercarriage and landing flaps, regulating the fuel pumps, propeller pitches and radiator flaps. My bomb-aimer lifts his left hand to indicate that everything is clear his side, and I check all my instruments while slowly closing on Hauptmann Peters. The other machines too have now joined us and we set course due west in a loose formation. Each of our aircraft carries 3,600 litres of fuel in its tanks, a reassuring amount.

To begin with, we do not fly very high, passing over shot-up villages and towns. Below us we can clearly recognise the half-finished but much-vaunted Weygand Line, a system of defensive positions that could not hold up the German advance. Here and there lie abandoned field guns and vehicles and other débris of war. But the most sorry sight is the roads crammed with refugees, a moving mass of humanity that has lost its way.

Hundreds of dead cows litter the fields, poor animals that died a horrible death just because there was no one to milk them. The whole scene is so desolate and dreadful that I completely forget I am on the way myself to participate in this inferno.

We cross the coast west of Le Havre to approach the target from the sea, hoping to elude enemy defences. No one can tell us exactly where the front line is, the situation is changing so fast. Le Havre is still burning in several places, although the town has been in German hands for some days. In the port are wrecks of several sunken vessels that look like so many toy ships. We keep over the middle of the Channel. To the left, we recognise details of the French coast, to the right we can see far into the English hinterland.

It is an odd feeling, being suspended in mid-air between two countries separated by this expanse of water.

Our formation levels off at 4,000 metres altitude and after a set elapsed time we turn south. Cherbourg should come into sight at any moment. Preparing for the coming attack, I haul back a bit to the rear and gain more altitude to observe the raid, before going into a dive myself. The big French port spreads out before us, and in no time we are over our target area. The Ju 88s ahead of me go over into a dive almost simultaneously while I still mark time. The point target assigned to me I have recognised at once, and cast a final glance around before the attack. This is also the first time I experience aimed AA fire: it does not seem all that dangerous – the dark clouds of shell explosions appear at best a good 50 metres from my aircraft. Apart from that, the AA fire is not very intense: my introduction to it is very gentle!

Quite calmly, I let the target slide into the Plexiglas* panel underneath my feet until it crosses the mark that indicates my pitch-over point. In the meantime I prepare my trusty kite for the forthcoming dive, carrying out the necessary procedures that have long become routine: set propeller blades at better climbing pitch, switch on auxiliary fuel pumps, shut radiator flaps, adjust altimeter and set contacts for a pull-out signal at 800 metres altitude. Jupp switches on electric power to set the bomb fuses and readies the automatic bomb release gear. Each one of us makes a final check of his harness-belts, and then I rotate the trimming wheels of all three axes to their diving marks. Everything is ready! But wait – somehow I've almost forgotten to switch on the reflector sight, to regulate the brightness of the aiming circle and to set the angle of sight – but it

* Trade name of German-type Perspex (Tr.)

only takes a few seconds to remedy this omission.

I throttle back the engines almost to idling revs and then pull the lever that activates the hydraulically-operated dive brakes and simultaneously sets the adjustable tailplane so acutely that my Ju 88 dips down her nose almost with a jerk. The next instant we are shooting down towards the ground. I keep my sight on the target, which grows visibly larger, and correct my diving angle with careful control movements. Another glance around – in fact, upwards, because that is where the horizon now is – all clear. The AA fire does not disturb me, at least I do not consider it dangerous, even when my Ju 88 dives through some black smoke-clouds left by exploding shells and the smell of burnt cordite penetrates the cockpit.

My dive is exactly according to the book, just as in training, when the hooter signals the bomb-release altitude. From now on, my aircraft must continue diving without any acceleration, at constant speed: I am not to correct anything, otherwise the bombs will hit the ground somewhere else.

But I come through in dazzling style. A light pressure on the red push-button release on the control column, a sudden jolt in the aircraft – and the bombs are away! The Ju 88 pulls out of its dive automatically and we are pressed into our seats with four to five-fold acceleration (four to five Gs). At this moment it is best to lean one's head against the backrest, otherwise nothing one can do will stop it being forced onto one's chest. Another phenomenon experienced at this pull-out stage is the momentary loss of consciousness known to us as the 'grey curtain', but within a few seconds we are fully intact again. By then, the machine is shooting steeply upwards with about 500 km/h (310 mph) on the clock, and I am pulling it into evasive manoeuvres. We are down into light AA gun range, and their red tracers are following uncomfortably close behind us. Moritz has a good view of the target from his ventral gun gondola and shouts with joy that we have hit the bull's eye.

And now to get away from here. I do not have to look for my companions who have dived before me: a furious AA fire of all calibres is indicating their course for all to see. This is greatly to my advantage because I can distance myself almost unmolested, even if I am forced to fly some rather mild evasive manoeuvres on the way.

All at once there's peace and quiet, and I can start thinking about the homeward flight. To begin with, I bring the whole aircraft into cruise flight condition and then set course to fly more or less in the wake of our approach flight.

It becomes one of those exquisite flights into the evening dusk, even more beautiful because we have passed our baptism of fire and in addition have the satisfaction of knowing that we have been successful.

I am the last to land back at Le Coulot. It is already twilight. Hardly any of the others have got away unscathed, and two crewmen are lightly wounded by AA shell splinters. The experienced hands talk of medium to heavy AA fire, something I could not judge as yet. Be that as it may, my tactics seemed to be correct.

16 June 1940

My second operational flight: five Ju 88s have to attack a bridge at Tours. Our formation is made up of a *Kette* (flight) consisting of Oberleutnant Stoffregen, Leutnant Mann and Unteroffizier Stahl, and a *Rotte* (separate pair), comprising Feldwebel Erkens and Unteroffizier Schröder.

This time we take off from our advanced field with fully loaded aircraft and I am sure we all wondered afterwards how we managed to get away as we did. My heavy machine rumbled and jolted so badly over uneven stretches on the ground that I thought our take-off would end in a crash. It was really a matter of touch and go when I finally managed to become airborne. The time was 1245 hrs when we began our steady climb to close in with the others and set our estimated course to the target. Our heavily-loaded aircraft seem to be rather swimming than flying in the air. There is 4/10 cloud, all cumulus, up to about 3,000 metres. We cannot see anything of the front line, which we cross on the way, but on the few roads we can spot through gaps in the clouds there's the same confusion as we noticed yesterday.

We have been warned to keep a sharp lookout for enemy fighters, but nobody bothers us. After some two hours' flying time, Tours appears spread out below to the left of us and we can clearly make out our target, a bridge spanning the River Loire, supported on several piers. Our reception by AA fire is quite warm, and the gunners seem to be shooting better and more intensely than their colleagues at Cherbourg yesterday. Our flight is the first on target. Stoffregen swings out westwards to attack from that direction, while Erkens and Schröder turn eastwards and then make a wide swing south, to come in that way. This splits the AA fire and gives us noticeable relief.

I repeat my tactics of yesterday, distancing myself to starboard rear so that I can first observe the proceedings and have the additional advantage of being able to commence my dive from the sun-up position. In the next instant my two front-rank men go head-over into dive almost simultaneously. Their trajectory is accompanied all the way down by bursting AA shells that leave an expanding cloud of dark smoke puffs, but I am still left in peace.

The French AA gunners are obviously on their toes: I am mentally keeping my fingers crossed – can I avoid their concentrated attention when I follow my companions on my own?

While banking into my target approach flight I have a chance of observing the bomb explosions of Stoffregen and Mann: both have narrowly missed the target. And then it is my turn, and a repeat of yesterday's play: calm approach flight at measured speed, preparation of the machine for the dive, exact setting of bomb release gear and propeller pitch. The target passes the red mark on the floor Plexiglass panel, and I pull the dive brake lever. The nose goes down, and we are on our way again! A quick glance around – everything is still peace and quiet in my corner: AA fire has moved to the south where Erkens and Schröder are just commencing their approach flight. Right – I can now concentrate on my own dive and aim very carefully. Suddenly a series of AA shells throw up their dark cloudbursts just ahead, immediately followed by a scream from Gross – we are hit! Without further ado I press the pull-out button on the port wall panel. This automatically terminates the dive, but does not release the bombs. The usual 'grey curtain', then blue skies again – is somebody hit? No! My engines are running normally and all instruments are indicating the way they should. What has happened then? An unusual noise in the cabin clears up the mystery at once: an AA shell splinter has shattered a Plexiglas panel, causing an unpleasant rumbling and whistling from the slip-stream, that seems to be all.

My mind is made up right away: we will repeat our attack!

However, to do so I first have to regain altitude. I ram both 'gas hammers' forward to squeeze the maximum climbing performance out of my engines. And yet everything seems to be happening so slowly! While we are straining for altitude, I can see both Erkens and Schröder nearing their tip-over point from the south, surrounded by furious AA fire. Once again, I climb into the sun without attracting any AA shells, and warn my crew to keep a sharp lookout for fighters. As the other two Ju 88s flick their tails up to start their attack dive, I have reached a good 2,000 metres altitude. I must attack at once, otherwise I'll have no chance of getting away unscathed on my own: down there they are waiting for just such a straggler!

I bank and begin my target approach. Everything goes well – I come out of the sun and still do not attract any attention from AA gunners. The play is repeated once more: below, the explosions of bombs dropped by my predecessors while I am concentrating on my approach flight, and then the dive. It is almost like a practice run, although I dive quite a bit lower than the usual pull-out altitude. The bombs fall – the 'grey curtain' – blue skies – and then nothing but away from there! After the pull-out, I push the control column forward to gain maximum speed, while Moritz reports a hit. And then the AA gunners are on us, but a bit too late; I manage to avoid any further damage with a series of wild evasive manoeuvres.

All of a sudden there is peace and quiet around us again. I readjust my Ju 88 to cruising flight and turn for home. While we were otherwise engaged the weather has turned sour and now bumps us around. There is a thunderstorm ahead of us and we have to change course to fly over Paris. A short while later we are over the historic battlefields of the First World War, and soon afterwards reach Le Coulot.

All the others except Leutnant Mann have already landed when I taxi to my parking space at 1710 hrs. The crews gather around and wait anxiously until it is obvious that Leutnant Mann can no longer be expected back: his fuel would have been exhausted.

The subsequent evaluation of our attack shows that Erkens and I have achieved such good hits that probably the bridge is now impassable.

In the evening we have a good serious drinking session with many speeches in the nearby village. The wine is good and our hosts in the local inn are most pleasant. It all helps us to forget the tensions of the day.

17 June 1940

They say France is nearing the end, and that we can soon expect an Armistice. This calls for another celebration, and we have just started it when we are ordered to get ready for another operation! It is to be an attack on a large concentration of ships in the Loire estuary. The actual operational orders arrive shortly afterwards; we have to take off at 1500 hrs.

This time we are flying in loose formation, fourteen Ju 88s with the Eagle insignia of our Geschwader on their noses. Once again we cross the old battlefields of the First World War and can also observe the after-effects of the present one. The approach flight seems endlessly long and after a while I fall back behind the formation to save the engines. The risk of being picked on as an especially enticing lone target seems comparatively small at this phase of the war – I would much rather have a pair of healthy engines as a precondition of getting back home again!

At the target I experience my first contact with fighters – French Moranes – but to begin with they do not attack me. The twisting and turning takes place at the other end of the estuary, and I can clearly see one Ju 88 going down with a smoking port engine. There are the ships! A vast fleet of freighters of all sizes lie scattered in the broad river estuary – there is no need for us to fly as far as the port of St Nazaire. Our reception is quite warm, with furious AA fire. As usual, I fall back a little and have a quiet target approach flight. All at once I hear Moritz's voice on the intercom: 'Fighters coming towards us!' – 'How far are they?' – 'There is only one, about 500 metres away!'

There is no time now for the finer points of dive-bombing. With a sharp movement on controls I tip my Ju 88 on its head and go down without bothering about dive brakes. Moritz reports that the Morane is following us. Now for it! The Ju 88 gains speed at a tremendous rate and we are soon diving at 600 and then 680 km/h (370 – 423 mph). I set my sights on a fat freighter, pull the nose of my Ju 88 up a bit, and then let go of the bombs. Now out of here!

With continuous control movements I pull the machine in a steep downwards bank that takes us out of the reach of light AA guns. I am still going at a high speed, while Moritz and Jupp keep reporting what the French fighter is up to. It is still following us, but seems unable to catch up.

The way things are this tenacious fellow is bound to catch me when I have to slow down near ground level. There is nothing for it but to start twisting and turning to throw him off his aim. A steep bank upwards temporarily gives me a bit of breathing space, but the Morane is soon back again and tries all kinds of tricks, helped by its higher level speed, to get into a firing position. The moment the French fighter steadies his aircraft, I throw my Ju 88 into a steep bank to port or starboard to shake him off, and the game begins again. All at once, as suddenly as the Morane had appeared it turns away. The French pilot had 'broken his teeth' trying to get my Ju 88 and now swings back again towards the big turmoil over the target area.

Relieved, we make speedy tracks for home base. The encounter had been rather hairy to say the least!

Naturally, due to the air combat there could be no question of observing our bombing results, and so my report on landing at the base was rather thin. However, the total success of our Gruppe is excellent: without losing a single aircraft we have achieved a large number of good hits, some of which can be mutually confirmed by several crews. Unteroffizier Geffgen was also intercepted by a French fighter but was not as fortunate as I: he collected more than 70 hits in his Ju 88 but still made it back to base all right. And not only that: due to shot-up hydraulics he made a first-rate belly landing perforce using his four 250 kg underwing bombs as skids – he could get rid of them because all his electric and mechanical release mechanisms had been shot out of action. Geffgen's landing was something I would not want to imitate: in his situation I would rather have baled out by parachute. I knew all about our bombs being 'safe' against damage by gunfire, but to skid along on four bombs? ... Who could tell if the heat caused by friction would not set them off? No, thanks!

Shortly after our landing, the news comes through that France has capitulated. We are over the moon with joy, and even the local

Belgian population joins us – most probably because they believe this means the end of the war, not because we have won it.

The guns fall silent at 1700 hrs. We hear that France has also made a similar offer to Italy, so it really is over. Soon afterwards instructions come through ordering us back to Perleberg tomorrow.

Somehow our celebrations that night are dampened, mainly because most of us are probably thinking about what is going to happen now. Most important of all, what is England going to do? More important to us, what do our leaders intend to do?

We also talk about the sense or absurdity of our last two operations. About Tours we know already that Erkens and myself succeeded in destroying the bridge at the very moment the last French troops were fleeing over it. As a result of our bombing our own troops could not cross the river to follow the enemy there! At the Loire, we dive-bombed and badly damaged a number of freighters one hour after the agreed armistice – not that we knew anything about it.

Really, I've no reason to modify my scepticism regarding the performance of our higher military leadership.

18 June 1940

We fly back to Perleberg late in the afternoon. Before that we pay a visit to Louvain and stroll through that beautiful town. The town hall in particular makes a great impression on us. Even today, one can still see traces of the First World War here and there. The local population is surprisingly friendly towards us and there are mutual congratulations on the end of the war against France. A young fellow tells us how astonished he and his friend had been about the armament and equipment of the German troops.

The propaganda disseminated in Belgium had the Germans so short of rubber they did not even have enough for car tyres, and our other equipment was supposed to be in a similar state.

My efforts to get a better crew have surprisingly quick success. As from today, I am taking over the former crew of our Gruppe commander: bomb aimer/navigator Hans Fecht, wireless operator Hein Hallert and air gunner Theo Goertz. Hans, a tall 25-year-old Swabian from Ludwigsburg, is an engineer and specialist on calculating machines by trade; Hein from Berlin is a student and is twenty-one years old; and Theo, also a student from Berlin, is just twenty, likes to take things easy, and shows a tendency to put on weight.

I have an opportunity to experience the incomparably better work of my new comrades already during the flight from Le Coulot to Perleberg. For their part, my new crew show their respect and appreciation of my flying abilities; it would seem that the commander was not a particularly good pilot.

Our next operations will be against England.

CHAPTER FOUR

Target London

25 August 1940: *Grove, Denmark*

Once again we had two months of home station life with the usual activities: handball games, instructions on the usual subjects, boredom and, again and again, training and practice flights. However, during this period I also managed to 'organise' four weeks' home leave for myself so I can't really complain!

In the meantime, an air battle on a scale previously unknown is raging over England. It is being said that the British are already on their last legs, but when one hears what the operational pilots – and in particular bombers crews – have to report, we're obviously still a long way from victory. The losses suffered by our bomber units must be terrible.

For that reason alone we cannot really understand why our Gruppe still has not been ordered back on operations. It seems odd to kick our heels here while other bomber crews are fighting to exhaustion.

Grove is a new airfield of vast dimensions. It has three concrete runways of over 1,200 metres length each, crossing in different directions. Each aircraft has its own covered dispersal pen, half-sunk into the ground. Although the accommodation consists of barracks, they offer every comfort and cannot be compared with other wartime buildings of this type. The system of communication roads and taxiways is many kilometres long – we have never seen anything like it. Work is still going on in every corner, and we are told they've sometimes had more than 800 people working on this airfield at the same time.

It is clear that we shall be taking part in the air combat over England from this base.

In view of the contradictions between the official news bulletin and the reports of our comrades flying on daily operations our mood is rather divided.

1 September 1940

Orders arrive for a major effort today: II and III Gruppen of KG 30 based on this airfield are to attack the RAF airfield at Driffield.

All preparations go according to plan, and the bombers – more than fifty Ju 88s – taxi out to the runway exactly on time. But it is not my day: my Ju 88 is withdrawn at the very last moment, because the boost pressure of the port engine registers certain irregularities. All my protests are in vain: the Technical Officer forbids the aircraft to take off, and we are left behind.

Over the target our crews experience all that we have heard from other formations flying these daylight raids for some time: a well-led and numerically strong fighter defence. The escorting German Bf 110 heavy fighters are delivered just as much 'on a plate' to the British Hurricanes and Spitfires as the Ju 88 bombers they were supposed to protect.

Our losses total eight Ju 88s with their crews: Hauptmann Brede, Leutnant Kiesser, Unteroffizier Brandt and Unteroffizier Bier from our Gruppe, and four other crews from III Gruppe. Those who were fortunate enough to get back were glad they had made it more or less in one piece. There were many wounded, and numerous hits in the aircraft. One pilot landed on two 'flat feet', without realising that his tyres had been shot through.

As a result, both Gruppen are only conditionally operational for some days and perhaps weeks.

2 September 1940

Sudden orders transferring our II Gruppe to Belgium. The new airfield is called Chièvre, near Mons. We take off individually whenever machines are cleared for flight. Of the thirty-six proud Ju 88s we had yesterday only fourteen are fit to fly.

We find the new base right away, although like Le Coulot it is nothing more than a large area of harvested fields. On touching down I have a blow-out in one tyre and manage with some difficulty to prevent a 'Californian crash'. I have to leave my machine in the middle of the field and we end up marching across the fields in the brooding heat to report at the command post: not the most pleasant of arrivals.

We are quartered in an old castle deserted by its owners. It is a bit down at the heel but otherwise quite comfortable. In the evening we pay a visit to the nearby village where a lot of beer and wine is consumed in a cheerful bar of sorts. The locals are quite willing to join in conversation and tell us we should beat the British as quickly as we can, so that the war will be over soon. Political subjects are avoided by both sides.

9 September 1940

An attack on London. During the last few days our aircraft have been operational over England almost every day, and with hardly any losses. The returning crews report successful attacks on British towns, airfields and, most recently, on London in particular.

Once again I have been left out of action. My Ju 88 became unserviceable exactly a week ago, when the inertia starter of the port engine disintegrated suddenly. This unexpected technical hitch again sentenced me to inactivity while the other crews amassed operational flights and experience. But today I am going along as well! I still have not got my own machine, and have to fly the oldest 'sledge' the Gruppe has, but nevertheless, I'm back in action again!

The whole Gruppe flies in close formation until we have to climb through a cloud cover, when the machines get scattered. There is also considerable icing, which makes things even more complicated. When the sun appears again I find myself with the leading flight and remain there. Why not?

Over Lille is our agreed meeting point with units from other Geschwader. Eventually there is an assembly of at least 200 bombers that gathers into some order and sets course for London. Soon afterwards we are joined by an escort of Bf 109s and Bf 110s. The cloud cover beneath us gradually breaks up so that Hans can navigate according to his map.

Flying as an individual in a formation made up of three bomber, two fighter and one Bf 110 Geschwader gives one a feeling of security. Wherever one looks are our aircraft, all around, a marvellous sight. Among ourselves we estimate that the total bomb load destined to fall on London soon afterwards amounts to at least 200,000 kg. And this has been going on for some days already. Poor London!

While crossing the Channel our formations sort themselves out. The fighters begin to fly a zig-zag course alongside, above and underneath us. The British Isles greet us with quite accurate AA salvos. This is the first time in the war that I am flying over the English coastline, confident and ready for the coming action.

The visibility is good, and we can even observe trains moving along the railway lines. Hans gives me a signal and points ahead. In the distance there are black smoke pillars reaching up to our altitude of 5,000 metres – that must be London.

Very soon we have reached the outer AA gun belt of the capital. The Brits are shooting unpleasantly well, and the whole formation becomes restless. It is now hardly possible to hold my position and I have to devote my whole attention to flying to avoid colliding with other aircraft. All this is completely new to me, and I have no idea how under these circumstances I'm going to follow my own tactics. There is nothing for it but to remain in the middle of the 'big heap'. The AA fire is furious, the shells are continuously exploding all around, above and below us. The surprising thing about it is that all our aircraft are flying on apparently unscathed. Apart from that the AA fire seems to me an indication that there are no fighters in our vicinity. I am scared of them like the plague, even if I have no other experience than the encounter over the Loire estuary.

With uncanny inevitability the whole big formation pushes forward over the great city. Ahead I can already see the first bombs falling, and then it is my turn to press the red release button: it is simpler in level formation bombing. The aircraft makes its usual jump of relief and we look down. The Thames bends, the docks and the whole colossal city lie spread out before us like a giant map.

Then come the explosions of our bombs which we observe while banking in a wide turn eastwards, then south. It must be terrible down there. We can see many conflagrations caused by previous bombing raids. The effect of our own attack is an enormous cloud of smoke and dust that shoots up into the sky like a broad moving strip. One cannot imagine that a town or a people could endure this continuous crushing burden for long.

Due to the increasingly stronger AA fire our formation has now disintegrated. After dropping their bombs each crew apparently tries to make off the best way they can. The previously solid formation has become more like a big herd. I try to get an overall view of the situation and search for a seemingly safer place for myself more by feel than anything else. It proves pretty soon that flying the Ju 88 has considerable advantages in a mixed formation of Do 17Z, He 111 and Ju 88 bombers: the Ju 88 has sufficient speed reserves to change our position and altitude freely.

Suddenly there are fighters among us. At first I take them for our own escorts and wonder about their tactics, twisting around among bombers in such a foolhardy way. Then I realise that they are British. Damn it, that is all we need! 'Hein, keep your eyes open, they are Tommies!' So much for peace and that sense of security in a big heap! There is tracer all around us, and a wild twisting turning air combat has broken out between our 109s and the Spitfires and Hurricanes. Now everything is happening right underneath us! I get away to hide in the thickest bunch of our bombers I can spot nearby, and warn my crew to inform me continuously and precisely about everything happening around us. At this time I am so fully taken up manoeuvring the plane for the best position that I simply cannot keep an eye on developments in the air as well.

Hein suddenly opens fire with his MG and makes me jump, but he himself is as calm as anything and only reports that, 'They have turned away!' He really has good nerves! Then I spot some parachutes to the left below us, and see a He 111 ahead of me going down in a steep glide streaming smoke. A few moments later I overtake another He 111 flying with one dead propeller. I feel sorry for the poor fellows, but there is nothing I can do.

All at once everything is quiet again. The Tommies have disappeared, and we are flying towards the French coast. It is over.

While I am eating my post-prandial sandwich which I always carry in the knee pocket of my flying suit, something that always calms me down, Leo taps me on the shoulder and shows me a broad oil slick glistening over the wing behind the starboard engine. A quick manipulation on the switch panel to check the oil situation shows that we have already lost 80 litres. That leaves only 10 litres in the oil tank, and means that I must immediately shut down the engine to avoid it seizing up. I let it run for a few more minutes but am forced to realise that there really is no alternative but to continue on one engine.

We are over the same 10/10 cloud cover as before with its icing up problems, but I must get through it. I dive in, hanging on instruments with my eyes and senses, trying to make up my mind which anomalies in the unusual situation are to be taken into consideration in one-engined flight. – 'Hans, external temperature?' – 'Plus two degrees' – 'Ice?' – 'Very slight!' Thank God, it is better than I expected!

Underneath us the clouds become darker, an indication that we are near the ground. We dive out of the cloud cover at about 400 metres, but where are we? Hans pokes me in the ribs and points to the right – an airfield! It is Amiens.

In the hope that the meagre supply of oil would last at least for the landing I restart the starboard engine and make the shortest landing turn I have ever flown in a Ju 88. We touch down, the wheels rumble over the air-field until we come to a stop and I can switch off the engines. Our first trip to London is over.

On foot we march along to the airfield flight control to report that our machine will have to be towed away due to a shot-up engine. Any further running will ruin it completely. Next, I go into the teleprinter office to send a message to Chièvres, informing them that we have landed here due to engine damage as a result of enemy action, and that it will probably be possible to repair the damage where we are. So much for the official part.

We are allocated quarters with some very nice people in a small place called Beauves. The word has quickly got around that we have force-landed here on the way back from England, and we become the centre of attraction in the village café, both for the few German soldiers stationed here, and all the local population. It is the same as we have already experienced at Le Coulot: the locals consider us the victims of our leaders, but at the same time they boundlessly admire our military achievements. In their eyes we are still heroes, and it is really touching how well they look after us.

12 September 1940
It could not be more lunatic than this! The repairs on our aircraft

were completed today and I make a test flight. What happens? Somehow or other in the flight, the dinghy gets out of its dorsal container on the fuselage, and everything is delayed by several hours.

While we are waiting for that dinghy business to be sorted out, a Ju 52/3m lands on the field and I recognise it as the transport machine from our Gruppe. We assume that it has called here to collect us, or at least to look after us in some way, but things take a different turn. A whole group of people climb out of the Ju 52. Inspector Dannenberg is the first to recognise us, and comes running across the field, shouting something we cannot understand. and then it dawns on us: apparently we've long since been reported as missing and written off! Our relatives have already been informed that we have not returned from an operational flight, and our belongings are packed and on the way to our families!

It appears that our teleprinter message never arrived at Chièvres, and consequently everything had run according to routine: inform the families, secure the private belongings, report the loss of the crew via proper channels, and so on.

I run to the local signals office at once and request a direct telephone connection with Chièvres, which I get surprisingly quickly, to report this mix-up, and ask Stoffregen, our new Staffelkapitän, to put the matter right. But it is already too late: our families have been informed that we are missing in action!

Superstition says that whoever has been mistakenly reported missing or killed in action can be sure of remaining alive. Well, I'd certainly like to believe it!

20 September 1940
Today we transfer to Gilze-Rijen in Holland. During the preceding eight days I have flown with our Ju 52 to exhaustion from one airfield to another in Germany, Denmark, Belgium and France 'on official business'.

The question of daytime raids on England now seems to have been settled somehow, either because our losses have been too high, or because we have not achieved the hoped-for successes, or because our formations simply need a respite: or probably, all three!

The new airfield is really nice, with concreted runways and

splendid accommodation in a monastery. And not only that: the cooking there is really fabulous.

We have no idea what the war has in store for us. The crews make the best of this unexpected interval, passing their time with sports, or going fishing or hunting. While all this is going I am flying daily with a Bf 108, practically without a break, on all kinds of impossible routes, carrying a right mixture of orders and other official papers. But for the war I could not wish for a better life as an airman-aerial postman!

25 September 1940
My fifth operational flight as part of the individual harassing attacks on London. We're now a bit more modest: it's not so much a matter of achieving some kind of success, but mainly to ensure there's at least an air raid warning in London.

However for us poor sausages it is anything but easy. During the previous large-scale raids one could to some extent hide inside the large formations, but flying alone, one is always exposed like a practice target to a well-coordinated defence organisation.

After pushing the throttle forward for take-off I mentally recite a quick prayer which includes two important points: 'Dear God, please let my two engines remain healthy, and see to it that there is bad weather – or at least a lot of nice thick clouds over London!'

On the way across the Channel we are flying over unbroken cloud cover – and are shot at by anti-aircraft guns. But they are our own: it would seem that they are always a bit bored and, after all, they do have to keep in training! That they cannot see anything does not come into it.

As the Devil would have it, the clouds underneath us start thinning out as soon as we are over the Channel. The nearer we get to the target the fewer clouds there are, so that in a fighter attack we are pretty well unprotected in the air.

All four of us are anxiously searching the sky around us for Spitfires. Sure enough, exactly at the spot where we could assume the sirens would begin announcing an approaching raid on London we see them: four fighters below us in a steady climb in our direction.

It does not take long for us to decide that there is nothing to be

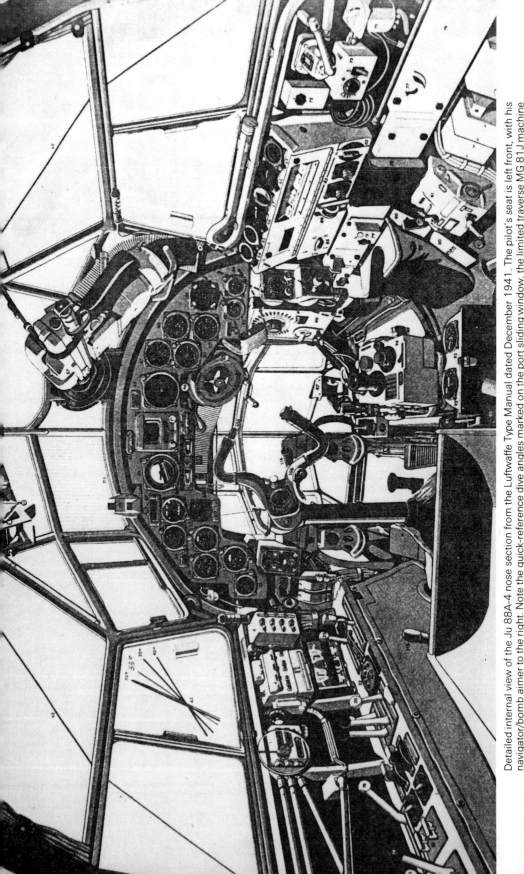

Detailed internal view of the Ju 88A-4 nose section from the Luftwaffe Type Manual dated December 1941. The pilot's seat is left front, with his navigator/bomb aimer to the right. Note the quick-reference dive angles marked on the port sliding window, the limited traverse MG 81J machine done here now. I break off our approach, tipping the aircraft on a wing and whipping round in the fastest turn of my life. All around us nothing but blue sky, and then Theo reports from his ventral gun position that the fighters are turning with us and coming closer. The nearest cloud seems almost out of reach. We are all nervous except Hans, who busies himself with his compass, course and distance-calculator and maps as if we were on a training flight. Theo reports that the fighters have split up in two pairs in an obvious manoeuvre to take us in a pincer. I give full throttle and aim for the nearest cloud. It becomes a race that I succeed in winning. Every pilot knows that the distance to a cloud is always less than it first seems, and although my mind recalls this piece of practical experience, the seconds until we finally dive into the cotton wool of the thin cumulus cloud seem endlessly long.

It is really high time, because according to reports from Theo and Hein the fighters were almost in firing position. Inside the cloud it is so bright that I know we will be through it and shoot out of the other side in moments. And then what? The British fighters – they are Hurricanes – have obviously recognised this too, and make no attempt to follow me. And then it is all light again and the other side of the cloud is there. There follows a flying game which, if played in sport, would have been no end of fun. In our case it is a game played for our skins!

My Ju 88 does not let me down, and every time one or two Hurricanes get into a firing position I succeed in diving back into the cloud, forcing the enemy to manoeuvre for another attacking position on the other side. How often we repeat this game of hide and seek I have no idea: all I know is that I hold on to 'my' cloud for dear life. Finally, using a favourable moment, I manage to jump to another, larger cloud floating in the southerly direction, and from there into even thicker cloud cover that we already met during our approach flight. I finally succeed in shaking off the fighters, but it was a close-run thing!

This is where Hans comes into his own. As if nothing had happened, he calmly gives me a new course to fly and explains it is in the direction of Hastings, where we can get rid of our bombs. I really wonder where this fellow got his nerves.

A few minutes of blind flying, then we dive clear of the clouds and see the ground. Ahead of us is a town, and Hans queries: the railway station? So be it. Everything is so peaceful, no ground defences of any kind. I make an approach according to the book, dive, aim and press the button. Theo reports that our bombs are falling and directs me after levelling off so that he can observe the explosions. The bombs are dead on the target!

The clouds take us in again, we pull through them and set course for home. We are flying into the evening dusk, and that means a night landing at our base. This will be something new: not only the first night landing with a Ju 88 for our Gruppe, but also a test to see if night flying and landing with this aircraft type are within the capabilities of the average crew. Until now, because of its various teething problems, the Ju 88 has been considered unsuitable for night operations. It will be up to us now to prove it one way or another.

Before we can even see the airfield illuminations, a radio message comes through informing us that the normal runway is out of action due to a crash, and that we should use a cross-runway then still under construction. This is going to be interesting!

I make an orientation flight across the field and then come in to land. Everything is clear and my first night landing with the Diva goes well. After touching down we are rolling out on the ground when suddenly there is a jerk on my port undercarriage, the kite goes down on her left knee, swings around a bit and then lies still. My good landing has ended in a crash! What has happened?

It does not take long to get the picture. While rolling on the ground my port undercarriage wheel ran into a heap of construction rubble and collapsed. This obstacle was on the left shoulder of the runway and could not be seen in the dark – it did not even have a warning lamp on it. The whole business is annoying, but there is nothing we can do about it.

While we are still standing around discussing the whole sorry affair with some technical personnel, along comes the Hauptmann himself with the new Staffelkapitän and makes the dust fly. Above all, he wants to know who the hell was that idiot pilot, and then proceeds to lambast me in a way that could hardly be improved as regards unflattering remarks – without allowing me to say a single word in explanation. This is really hard, as I have just gone through

Peter W. Stahl and his crew shortly before an operational flight in autumn 1940. From l. to r. Theo Goertz (ventral gunner), Hein Hallert (radio operator), the author, and Hans Fecht (navigator/bomb aimer).

Ju 88A-6 balloon barrage destroyer. The total weight of the balloon cable fender and the trimming ballast in the rear fuselage amounted to 380 kg (838 lb), making the aircraft very unwieldy in combat. Intended to free the way for the following bombers, this adaptation of the standard Ju 88A-5 saw only brief operational service.

Gilze-Rijen, autumn 1940: a KG 30 aircrew just back from an operational flight over England. In the centre: Oberfeldwebel Mang, the Chief Mechanic of 4./KG 30.

a pretty nasty experience and apart from everything else, do not feel responsible for the crash in any way. Well, let bygones be bygones!

5 October 1940

I and my crew have been transferred to 6.Staffel. Hauptmann Wieting gives me a wink when I formally report to him as my new Staffelkapitän. No words are needed after the incident of 25 September.

CHAPTER FIVE

Night Raids on London and Coventry

Editor's note:
Written as diary entries at the time, the following passages clearly indicate that Luftwaffe bomber crews were not aware of British detection equipment that could track their aircraft no matter how they changed their course and altitude, never mind engine revs. Early British air defence relied on sound detection; this was soon superseded by the development of radar devices.

7 October 1940
Night raid on London 0130-1410 hrs. The Luftwaffe has changed its tactics. We are no longer flying in large closed formations or even singly in daytime against the British Isles because the losses have become unbearably high. Instead, the aim of wearing down the enemy is now to be achieved by raids of larger formations at night, in exactly the same manner as the British have already tried experimentally over Germany. There is even some talk of retaliation.

It is pitch-black as we fly into the night. All this is something quite new for us, and that is why we have made especially thorough preparations. For navigational aids we have light and radio beacons. Their positions and identification signals are known to us, and Hans makes a really good job of it all. Already, after flying over the second radio and light beacon on the island of Schouwen we are able to determine the wind direction and speed accurately, and make the necessary course corrections.

We can just see the Dutch coast below us as we fly out over the sea. The flashing light with the identification 'YW' is visible for quite some time, while I am continuing to climb steadily. We have been instructed to determine our own bearings for further navigation, the procedure being to tune in to known radio beacons with our direction-finder and then measure the direction relative to these transmitters. These values are then transferred onto a map where the points of intersection of any two such base lines would indicate our position at the time. Accurate observation of the elapsed time also makes it possible to calculate our true ground speed* and estimate the time to the target.

Then I notice that Hans seems to have forgotten a minor point from his lessons, and give him a hand. It is obvious that his previous captain, now at the War Academy, could not have known much of these things – perhaps he had not considered it important for his career. But it is different for us. Both Hans and I are enjoying this figure work. We communicate in sign language although we could easily have talked to each other via our throat mikes. But we find it better the simple way.

We arrive over the British coast right on the dot, and are greeted by searchlights which seem to be meandering in a desultory fashion around the sky. Even when they do light up one of our aircraft they do not hold it, but continue playing their searching game. We are flying at 7,000 metres, and our machine has been sprayed sooty black; it would seem that in this garb we are not visible to the searchlights. That sets our minds at rest, and I continue along the planned route north of the Thames. Ahead the sky is lit up by anti-aircraft fire, and it is soon like a thunderstorm all around us as well. But it is not all one-sided: we can see uninterrupted flashes on the ground, the explosions of bombs dropped by our companions.

One can easily tell the difference between anti-aircraft guns and bomb explosions: while the guns produce only a short flash, a bomb-explosion initially gives off a brighter flash, which then slowly burns out. At least that is how it looks to us from our height.

On the way back, after having dropped our bombs in the target area, we are caught by the anti-aircraft guns and this time they seem to be aiming directly at us. In no time at all we are exposed to a furious fire that forces me to fly some violent evasive manoeuvres. However that does not seem to help any, and then I realise that they are not shooting at individual targets but are firing a barrage, covering a predetermined space in the sky in the hope that one shell

---

* An aircraft has three main horizontal 'speeds': IAS, indicated air speed (from instruments); TAS, true air speed, speed through the air – which might be 300 mph against a 50 mph wind, leaving a GS – ground speed-of 250 mph. (The wind may also be setting the plane off sideways!)

would hit something. The deadly flashes appear at all heights around us and the minutes seem to be dragging endlessly. We turn south and then east, and manage to get out of the shooting in one piece.

'Hans, give us a course for home!'

'Fly 105 degrees for a bit, I still have to calculate the correct heading!'

I throttle back our engines and begin slowly to lose height. We are still over the British mainland and have to keep our wits about us. But all goes well and soon we cross the coast, marked by a line of searchlights. It almost looks as if they are waving us good-bye.

Then Hans gives me the correct bearing, and Hein asks if he can play some music. Why not? He switches on Radio Hilversum, and accompanied by cheerful entertaining sounds we cross the North Sea.

The weather is fine at Gilze-Rijen, so we land without any difficulties. It was a good sortie: all our comrades return to base. But even so the strain of this night raid shows on their faces, especially those of the younger crews. We are really glad when at long last we can crawl into our beds. The dawn is already breaking.

10 October 1940

London once again. Take-off 0245 hrs, landing back at the base 0610 hrs. The night is divided into minutes and each bomber Geschwader receives its share. Within a Geschwader, every single minute is allocated to one particular crew indicating when it is expected to be over the target. Our take-off times are fixed accordingly and any deviation would upset the whole operational plan.

We make it this time. The anti-aircraft fire is much more unpleasant than the previous night, and we only just manage to get through. A number of other aircraft are hit, and some are damaged quite badly. Two crews of 4.Staffel fail to return and are posted missing.

14 October 1940

Unusual – a daytime harassment raid on London. We take off in beautiful sunny weather at 1530 hrs, our orders being to cause an air raid alarm in London at the very least. Naturally, I am also given specific orders to attack a target of some importance, some locks in the dock area. Nevertheless, it must be evident even to the higher Luftwaffe command that a single bomber could not carry out this task with any real hope of success. The idea is simply to have air aid sirens howling in London 24 hours a day. It may sound good in theory but we have no doubt that this will cause us operational crews a lot of hardship and casualties.

15 October 1940

Another night raid on London. Take-off time 1925 hrs, landing back at the base 2220 hrs.

By now all the bearings, radio and light beacons, anti-aircraft zones and peaceful sections along the whole route are well known to us. After the pre-flight briefing Oberleutnant Wolf sums it up in a few words: 'It is the same old tour today. We have been allocated the target area A, and all take-off times are on the flight plan. Before that there's coffee, afterwards a good stew. Have a good trip!'

The weather on the way out is fine. We climb steadily while crossing the North Sea and arrive over the British Isles at 5,000 metres. We continue gaining altitude while flying towards the target, which is easily recognisable due to the massed anti-aircraft fire in the sky. All the signs are that this is going to be a hard night, right from the start. The number of searchlights that greet us on the coast is immense: we have never seen anything like it before. There seem to be hundreds of anti-aircraft guns along our route, and we do not have any peace for one minute. I try every trick in my book, every anti-aircraft evasion manoeuvre I know, but in vain: the explosions are the closest I have ever experienced. Even Hans becomes restless, which is most unusual.

We are just about to top the 7,000 metres mark when, flying another evasive turn, I suddenly became aware of the reason why they are shooting so well tonight: our aircraft is pulling along a beautiful contrail flag ... A good pointer to the anti-aircraft guns crews, practically indicating an individual target to shoot at! Instantly I throttle back the engines and begin losing altitude in steep spirals, going down to about 3,500 metres before continuing towards London. Sure enough, the familiar play of searchlights and

Gilze-Rijen airfield in autumn 1940. This Luftwaffe bomber base in the Netherlands was one of the most modern and best equipped at the time. Its camouflage was so effective that RAF bombers regularly raided the dummy airfield a few kilometres away.

A damaged Ju 88A-5 after a belly landing at Gilze-Rijen. The 'stubble field' was artificially laid to deceive aerial reconnaissance.

seemingly desultory anti-aircraft fire is back again. Like this we fly over the target, drop our bombs after careful aiming, and are able to observe the explosions before turning back.

When we finally leave the British coast with its waving searchlights behind us and fly out over the sea I feel very pleasantly relieved.

We are the last to land. This time three of our crews are missing. Our detailed combat report induces Hauptmann Hass, the commander of our Gruppe, to single us out for special praise. This is all thanks to Hans, who has carefully marked all observed bomb explosions according to time and position, throughout my evasive twists and turns in the raging anti-aircraft fire. Granted, the night was so light that from our altitude of only 3,500 metres we could see every detail on the ground – but one had to have the nerves of a Hans Fecht calmly to jot down accurate notes on his map, under the circumstances we were in. His self-control really amazes me.

16 October 1940

London again! During the day I have been given the task of training some young, newly arrived crews. All of them need a thorough schooling before they can be sent on difficult night flights, and I am one of the three chosen instructors.

The weather is not all that good and we are hoping for a free night, but it is not to be. The operational orders come through at 1700 hrs: another night raid on London. My take-off time is set for 1835 hrs. Soon after becoming airborne my Ju 88 is swallowed up by clouds and I have to fly blind. Keeping a wary eye on instruments, I keep climbing slowly. We navigate by taking bearings on known radio beacons and broadcasting stations. Both Hans and I are fully engaged determining our actual position and the compass-bearing we have to fly. The aircraft develops slight icing-up and I decide to climb through the freezing zone. At 6,000 metres altitude the external temperature has dropped to −30°C, but the icing-up has stopped. It is cold in the cabin, a constant fog of fine ice needles dusts in through every small crack in the cockpit glazing. Cloud still surrounds us.

I level off when it seems hopeless to climb through the cloud cover. I dare not go lower because I fear that layers of wetter air would cause heavy icing-up; we just have to remain at this altitude.

During our approach flight to London it becomes almost spooky in our glazed housing. The searchlights have lit up the clouds so we are flying blind, and we feel as if we are hanging in our fuzzy surroundings, sitting inside a white cottonwool ball, with no idea what is happening above and below us. I have flown blind a lot in my time, but I have never been exposed to this kind of situation. I have to concentrate really hard – 'to pull together my whole brain', as we used to say, to avoid making any errors. And that takes nerve! My sole wish is to be out of here, and quick.

In this night the Tommies have made what I consider to be a mistake by firing their AA guns in addition to using searchlights. The explosions of AA shells in the clouds around us provide welcome points of reference to my eyes and my brain: the gradual crescendo of AA shell explosions shows clearly that we are near our target area. Without any sight of the ground we can only drop our bombs according to this indication and our own navigational calculations.

Our task completed, we turn back on a home course. There are no problems and our flight over the British coastline is clearly indicated by the farewell of the searchlights. When passing through the temperature line around zero degrees we experience very heavy icing-up, so intense that we lose our aerial mast while the fuselage is drummed by pieces of ice shed by the propeller blades. I start losing altitude as quickly and steeply as I dare to get into some warmer air. We level off at just 100 metres over the Channel, still without sight of the water, but at least the external temperature is now +5°C. Gradually, the ice thaws out and I can breathe more easily.

I have to approach our base blind, and land safely in foggy haze in the pitch-black night. Most of the other crews had to be diverted to various alternate airfields.

Our losses amount to four Ju 88s with their crews, including Hauptmann Hass. This is a heavy blow, because to me this officer was an example in every way. He had it in him to do great things and was a wonderful human being. He possessed modesty, intelligence, discretion and bearing in a measure one seldom comes across in a person. We assume he has fallen victim to the treacherous icing-up which is seldom encountered in such density as last night.

There are two crashes on the airfield during landing operations,

A nose-over that had a better ending than expected.

This Ju 88A-5 cracked its port undercarriage leg during a night landing at Gilze-Rijen after an operational sortie over England.

although the crews are fortunate to escape without serious injury. In addition, Oberleutnant Baumbach* and Feldwebel Timm literally fell out of the clouds onto the bleak landscape while flying blind, but Fate was kind to them: both machines were totally destroyed but the crews survived.

While on the way by bus to our quarters we discuss the question, in view of the known unfavourable conditions, of how daft it is to send out hundreds of aircrews by night without any hope of reasonable results, and run the risk of having heavy losses simply on account of the bad weather. One of us comes up with what is probably the correct reason:

'What do you think, how many new generals does the Luftwaffe add to its ranks after each such shit operation?'

'You mean shit generals, not shit operations!' somebody else adds, and we fall silent. It does make one think.

And tomorrow, the communiqué of the armed forces high command will state that our brave aircrews have flown another major operation and despite bad weather conditions have inflicted devastating blows on various vital targets. Our own losses were only 'minimal'!

18 October 1940
The weather is too bad to fly. We play table tennis or lie about somewhere.

19 October 1940
I ferry one Ju 88 to Perleberg for a major overhaul. We are fêted by our old acquaintances and given special treatment in every way.

23 October 1940
The weather's been so bad during the last few days that it is only today we can fly from Perleberg back to Gilze-Rijen. Just in time to participate in another raid on London! We take off at 1845 hrs, and land back at the base at 2100 hrs. It must be really horrible to live in London now. The bombs are raining down night after night: the

---

* Subsequently to become the most successful anti-shipping expert flying the Ju 88, and ending the war as Oberst (Colonel) and commander of KG 200. Werner Baumbach lost his life flight testing an Avro Lancaster bomber in Argentina on 20 October 1953. (Tr.)

first Luftwaffe bombers appear in the evening dusk, the last, early in the morning.

Tonight, instead of the set approach route I tried to fly in further north, in the Norwich area, but here too the ground defences by AA guns and searchlights are uncomfortably strong and dangerous. Conditions over London are the same as usual. We are forced to bomb blind, guided only by the reflection of conflagrations on the clouds beneath us. Our landing at Gilze-Rijen is again quite difficult.

24 October 1940
With a Ju 52/3m to Uetersen, where I have to collect a Bf 108 liaison aircraft.

14 November 1940
From 26 October until yesterday we have been in Germany with our brave old 4D + HP. It was to have been a short business of only a few days, but then fate took a hand and prolonged our stay.

What happened was that our Ju 88 was fitted with additional armour plating at Gilze-Rijen and had to be flown to Germany to re-compensate its compass errors. These 'compensation flights' are always carried out to airfields in our homeland so that the crews can have a day or two's additional home leave and rest. It was a very good arrangement and worked both ways: the crews were happy, and the Staffel and Gruppe commanders were always pleased when they could report lower figures for operationally available crews to their superiors. It seems at HQ people are so far removed from the war that they no longer think of human beings but only of figures. That more and more operational crews are reaching the limits of their nerves and strength is ignored.

We chose Perleberg for our flight back home, and arrived there in good time. After landing, the technical personnel found something wrong with one of our engines, and the matter was apparently so serious that the whole engine unit had to be changed. As a result, we had two days to visit our families. Then some more defects were discovered in the aircraft, so in the end we had a real 'unscheduled' home leave that lasted almost three weeks. It was an unexpected present, and of course we made the most of it.

Yesterday we reported back to our Staffel, and today we are 'on' again. The operation carries the cover-name 'Mondschein' (Moonlight).

In the evening dusk we make a short hop to Eindhoven, one of our neighbouring bases, where our machines are loaded with mines. These are ordinary naval mines which are now to be used against land targets. The LM-A (*Luftmine-A*) weighs 500 kg, and the LM-B, 1,000 kg. They are shaped like big barrels and are intended to float down onto the target under parachutes, but nobody seems to know much about these things. The same goes for the target, which is only revealed during our operational briefing – it is Coventry.

My take-off time is fixed for exactly 2015 hrs. It is a beautiful night with marvellous clouds lit up by the moonlight, which makes night flying a particularly enjoyable experience. My Ju 88 carries a load of one LM-A and one LM-B, and we are told that tonight's operation will be the heaviest night air-raid ever flown against a target in England.

We can already see the furious anti-aircraft fire when some way off the British coast. Could they have suspected something? It is most unusual because we have never experienced such defensive effort in this particular area. But then, we have not been here for three weeks and a lot of things can happen in that time.

A red reflection is visible beyond the horizon before we even cross the coast – that must be the target! There is no need for navigation now and I vary my approach route to avoid areas with particularly massed anti-aircraft fire.

The nearer we get to the target, the more we become aware that absolute Hell must be let loose down there. Mines released by earlier aircraft explode in regular series, and one can almost tell by the clock at what intervals the bombers fly over the target. As we get nearer, the anti-aircraft fire becomes thicker and it seems as if thousands of searchlights are in action, even more than I have noticed over London. The approach flight through this blazing inferno, punctuated by the explosions of anti-aircraft shells, seems endlessly long and I am forced to fly evasive manoeuvres time and again. But what we experience over the target itself surpasses everything one could possibly imagine. The whole town seems to be ablaze, and we are only in the vanguard, a large number of our bombers are still on the way, their navigation problems solved by the fiery reflection in the sky. In addition, the target is also lit up by flare-bombs that flash at irregular intervals.

With throttled-back engines I begin a glide towards my allocated target area near the outskirts of Coventry. Below us, we can now clearly recognise whole burning streets and larger conflagrations. Suddenly my Ju 88 is met by accurate anti-aircraft fire that forces me to turn away, but this is only temporary. I mark time until the exploding shells begin to concentrate around another aircraft, and then use that moment to go into a steeply inclined flight at high speed towards my release point. On the way I have to fly over the burning town once more, and when I finally drop my mines at exactly the right spot we are just 2,000 metres high. That seems a bit too low for Hans who pokes me in the ribs several times and points to the altimeter.

We are in an inferno that almost defies description. Beneath us is red blazing heat giving rise to an enormous smoke cloud that in turn is lit up and made glowing by the fires below, making the whole airspace into a giant fireball. Explosions from bombs, anti-aircraft gunfire and their shells flash below, above and all around us. It really feels like flying through Hell itself!

We lose all sense of time and space, but I simply cannot leave the gruesome spectacle below us until I have flown another wide circle around it before asking Hans to give me the course for home. To be on the safe side I again climb to a respectable altitude until we cross the British coastline. I then begin an extended glide over the North Sea to our base.

The returned crews are in an exalted mood, partly because we are glad to have got away with it once more and partly because we have taken part in an almost unimaginable experience.

Only two aircraft from our Gruppe are missing; they were flown by youngsters from other Staffeln.

15 November 1940
With the good old 'Heinrich'* to London. I have to fly almost the

---

* Luftwaffe aircraft (except single-seat fighters) were usually known by their individual letter within the Staffel which was pronounced according to the

whole distance blind in cloud but we now have a new method that enables us to make the approach flight and achieve aimed bombing through cloud cover. It is known as '*Knickebein*' ('Knock-knee' or 'Crooked Leg') In this method, concentrated radio beams are directed over England from the east and south so that their point of intersection is over the chosen target. I fly along the guide-beam from the east and, if I am accurately on course, I hear a continuous tone in my earphones. If I happen to deviate to the left, I hear Morse 'dots'; a deviation to right results in 'dashes'. The point of intersection with the radio beam from the south is indicated by a tone in a different key.

The whole procedure worked very well indeed. However, my own impression was that the British AA guns were shooting even better tonight than ever before. Could it be that they had already discovered our new technique and are now concentrating their AA fire on these guide-beams?* Be as it may, I am overjoyed when I can finally press on the bomb-release button and make myself scarce as quickly and quietly as I possibly can to the south.

All in all, it was quite strenuous blind flying against really mean defences! We took off at 2250 hrs and landed back at the base at 0135 hrs.

16 November 1940

The same old 'milk run' to London again. At the same time we are to test a new navigational method working on the long-wave band and known as *Elektra*. This method seems excellent and considerably eases our navigational tasks.

Once again, the target is hidden by cloud cover so that again we have to determine our bomb-release point according to navigation and the reflected fires and explosions below.

Tonight I am trying out another approach route: I fly directly

---

contemporary service radio-telephone phonetic alphabet. In this case the full code designation was 4D + HP (4D = KG 30; H = 'Heinrich', individual letter within the Staffel; and P = 6.*Staffel*) (Tr.)

* The '*Knickebein*' radio guidance beams were detected by the British Intelligence before the Coventry raid and simulated to lead the Luftwaffe bombers astray shortly afterwards. (Tr.)

Gilze-Rijen, autumn 1940. The difficult night landings after hard operations over England and many hours in the air took their toll. Note the overpainted KG 30 insignia, propeller spinners and all lighter-coloured markings on the fuselage to assist night camouflage.

Two 1000 kg (2205 lb) LM 1000 aerial mines ready for loading into a Ju 88A. The rounded caps covered the parachutes which were released at a predetermined altitude. By readjusting their fuse mechanism these mines could be used both against shipping and land targets.

along the formerly dreaded course of the Thames estuary and we are relatively unmolested by the British AA guns. Compared to the previous nights, it was almost a relaxing flight. I remind my crew to keep our experience to ourselves, otherwise it will be the end of this cosiness in no time.

19 November 1940

Tonight we are free and can ease up a bit. This results in a real 'bomber feast' in our quarters. The strain of the last few weeks is off-loaded spontaneously and in truly extravagant style. Our officers too join in, except for the Staffelkapitän of 5.Staffel of course. But nobody even bothers to think that tomorrow night we'll have to fly to England again and we should be glad to have some rest tonight at least. Who cares!

The main subject is flying in all its variations – including of course war and our operational flights. We can hardly consider the sense or absurdity of it all. For we have too many problems ourselves, most of all, sheer survival, and only secondarily, success. But there is a minority to whom the emphasis is the direct opposite. As for these fellows we say that they are suffering from 'neck disease', meaning they are squinting for a Knight's Cross around their necks. Well, there are careerists in every profession!

We sing and shout until we are hoarse. In the middle of our loud merriment the door opens and Gefreiter Völling from our Orderly room runs in to announce that Feldwebel Willy Schulz is missing. The noise dies down at once, and we are serious again. Willy was sent out on a harassment operation to Southampton, together with Heinz Bruck. On return, Bruck reported furious AA defence around the target. It seems that Willy was probably shot down, because after the raid there was no reply to repeated attempts to contact him by radio. And now his time was up, he could no longer be airborne.

20 November 1940

We are searching for Willy. I receive my orders to take off still the same night of our party and arrive in the area where the search is to commence at first light. The weather is extremely bad, with low-hanging clouds and stormy winds. I fly out, very close to the English coast, and am occasionally shot at. The sea just underneath us is boiling, the strong wind whips off the froth from the wave-heads. A dinghy could not possibly survive in these conditions. I fly on nevertheless, until I have only just enough fuel left in my tanks to get back to base.

Our comrades are waiting for us at the command post. Hauptmann Wieting is grey in the face; none of the men has slept a wink. Willy was an outstanding comrade and an example to us all, and we miss him terribly. His crew were Heinz Schmidt, Sepp Dachauer and Achim Schätz. I am dead-beat.

CHAPTER SIX

The Blitz Continues

23 November 1940

Something completely new: minelaying in the Thames! My aircraft is loaded up with two LM-B mines. We know these things already from the Coventry days, but this time they are intended for their proper element, water.

At daybreak, shortly before we taxi to our take-off position, an engineer pays a visit to each aircraft, opens a small flap in the mine and fixes something inside. It is obvious he makes certain adjustments, but they are so secret that we are not permitted to know about them.

It is broad daylight when we arrive in our target area. Needless to say, we are as tense as can be. At very low altitude I fly towards Margate which is our starting point. From then on we continue by compass and stopwatch in a northerly direction, towards our target area. The Thames estuary is so broad here that one cannot see the other bank. The water is mostly very shallow, with only a few deeper channels suitable for larger ships. It is these channels that we will mine now. I have no reference points to help find the target area other than our compass and the clock. I press my Ju 88 down to just over the water surface to avoid being spotted, and pull up to the necessary release height only just before the estimated target stretch. Hans sees a chain of buoys which evidently mark the navigable water. These fit in exactly with our own calculations, and I release our mines. The aircraft makes a jump to show us it is suddenly 2,000 kg lighter, and I spiral down to get back to the water surface again as quickly as possible.

We can see clearly that the parachutes carrying our mines are floating down towards their intended place – our task is completed.

With full throttle I fly out towards the open sea and calm down only when we feel certain we are outside the range of Spitfires.

24 November 1940

Everything has gone barmy today. The weather is absolutely thick, but they want to send the whole Gruppe to attack London! Fortunately our CO succeeds in altering the order at the very last moment when the crews are already sitting in their machines, ready to go: it is agreed that only a few 'older' crews should fly this operation.

As a result Baumbach, Timm, Bohg and myself are chased out of the place. The night is pitch-black, with sleet and clouds right down to the ground.

Over London we observe a new trick for the first time: large dummy fires in various places outside the town, but none of us fall for it. After all, we know our way around here pretty well by now and, apart from that, we also know what a real fire in a town looks like.

On the other hand, our landing back at the base is nothing short of a real flying feat, despite the radio beam-assisted landing procedure now installed. Once again, Baumbach and Timm fall out of the sky outside the airfield, fortunately without any serious injury to the crews. Timm's Ju 88 came to rest in a large heap of straw and burned out completely. We wonder if the obvious lessons will be learned from this mess. It is absolute madness to attempt operations with average crews at night in such weather conditions. But somewhere or other there sits another character who wants to be a colonel or a general!

It is seldom that I am as glad to be back on the ground as tonight.

28 November 1940

With 'Emil'* to Liverpool, my own machine being overhauled. Once again, we take off into the night, and the red lamps of the airfield illuminations are left behind us. I have tuned the revs of both engines to match, and the instruments show normal values. Each one of these take-offs with an overloaded aircraft at night is

---

* See previous footnote re individual letters of aircraft within a Staffel. (Tr.)

tough on the nerves. The muscles in my buttocks relax only after the undercarriage has been retracted and the aircraft has gained sufficient speed for me to pull up the flaps and change into a steady climbing flight. There are times after such take-offs when I feel I've completed half the operational flight already.

As on most occasions, I am climbing blind and first set my eyes on stars at 3,000 metres altitude. While flying through the clouds we run into some ice that removes our radio aerial mast, an experience we've had before. Despite the starry sky everything is pitch-black around us. Hans busies himself with the direction-finding device, and gives me course corrections. We really have a long trip ahead of us tonight and I fly as economically as possible. We reach the English coast at 5,000 metres altitude and note strong AA fire to the left of us.

There are other aircraft in that area, possibly from another Geschwader, and we are again lucky to have hit a peaceful 'strip' for our arrival. After our landfall we are faced with a long overland flight right across the British Isles to the west coast. Numerous searchlights finger the air, and time and again the British AA guns feel out for us. When it becomes too uncomfortable I turn away for a while. Other machines are also flying somewhere in the area and are being shot at by the AA guns which helps me to get a good picture of the situation and pick my flight-path accordingly.

On reaching the west coast the AA defences become notably stronger. From the contours of the coastline we recognise that we are too far south and have to fly quite a distance northwards until I can faintly make out the River Mersey ahead of us. Apart from several dummy conflagrations and furious AA fire there is not much happening in the target area, but it takes us some effort to find our specific target, the port itself. Finally we are over it, I press the bomb release button and Emil can make its relief jump – our task has been completed.

Our return flight is very long and tiring against strong headwinds. The continually improving British AA defences do their part, so that we arrive at Gilze-Rijen completely exhausted. At the command post I see the steady changing appearance of the green and yellow faces of returning aircrews. We all have just one wish, to get to bed as quickly as possible. A quick look round to see if our best friends are still with us, and away. If any of the others are missing, we will get to know soon enough next morning.

Our take-off was at 2305 hrs, landing back at Gilze at 0410 hrs on the morning of –

29 November 1940

I wake up shortly after midday following a long healthy sleep. We have long since got used to having our breakfast in the early afternoon. The kitchen personnel too have adapted themselves to this pattern and do not mind the gap of several hours between the 'early wakers' and the 'late sleepers'.

A favourite subject among the pilots is their crews. Each one of us has apparently the best bomb-aimer, the nimblest wireless operator and the most original air-gunner. This is not really surprising when one considers that the four men of a Ju 88 crew are harnessed together in situations and under conditions that cannot be compared with anything else.

Herbert Bohg is on leave. We expect an operational order for tonight. My machine is undergoing the periodical 150-hour inspection so I have to fly Herbert Bohg's 'Bruno'. We sit around, and everybody is keeping himself occupied somehow, but one can feel the restlessness, the unspoken question: what will the night bring? Every time the door opens we start up and are glad when it is not Gefreiter Völling from the Orderly Room who usually comes in to announce the briefing for forthcoming operations.

The strain on our nerves during these free hours is at least as great as during an operational flight; that is the way we feel.

The order comes through in the late afternoon; another attack on London. This, in my book, is the least of all possible evils, because the flight will be shorter. We have a new moon, and it is a starry but still pitch-black night. The weather all along the route is excellent, without any problems. I fly along my proven 'southern lane' route again and, in fact, we are hardly shot at during our approach flight and only a few searchlights are active. But things are quite different over London, the sky is alive with hundreds of exploding AA shells all around us. Not only that: tonight they seem to have got not only our correct altitude but also our speed and lateral position! The shells burst ahead and behind us and any attempt at evasion seems

The author at the controls of his Ju 88A late in 1940.

pointless. Things are so bad that I catch myself several times wanting to give up, drop the bombs blind into the night and get out of here. but I persevere. The final target approach flight seems endlessly long until we can release our bombs. Knowing my stubborn bomb-aimer, Hans, I have no doubt in my mind they would be on target; all I want now is to get away as quickly as possible.

With full throttle I go steeply down and homewards – and then it happens: a blinding flash, it looks like we are hit! With one movement I pull up our Ju 88 and cast a quick glance at the instruments: everything seems normal. Thank God! Another check shows that nothing seems to be damaged in the aircraft, and there are no injuries among the crew. Fortune smiled on us again!

We fly over the coast, direction North Sea. I throttle back and slowly begin to lose height, and we all breathe easily again. Everything around is peaceful, and only the quiet stars are dotting the sky above us.

On levelling off, I pull back the throttle levers and am faced with a non-cooperative port engine which continues to run at full throttle . It is obvious that a shell splinter must have dropped the throttle controls and I now have a runaway engine. No aero-engine can last for long at full boost, so I switch it off and continue on my still healthy starboard engine.

The Ju 88 flies slanting in the dark night but we are on our way home. I contact Gilze by radio and request them to notify our own AA guns along the Belgian-Dutch coast that one of our aircraft in distress will fly low along the coast northwards. Naturally, with a sick kite on my hands I have immediately given up my planned course towards the North Sea and taken the shortest cut across the Channel. Ahead of us some searchlights finger the sky, but they are our own this time, and we are glad to see them. On approaching nearer we fire off the current daily identification flares, but the searchlights continue beaming right into our faces. Another lot of identification flares follow, but there is no reaction. Suddenly, light AA guns open up at us and I am forced to fly a dangerous evasive manoeuvre over the stopped engine.

And this deadly game of searchlights and light AA guns follows us all along the coast. In the end, my crew give up firing the identification flares and start shooting back with their machine-guns in earnest. We are so incensed that we are actually hoping we have hit some of those silly AA dopes!

I have no idea why such impossible mix-ups always seem to affect our AA artillery units. There are hundreds of similar stories where our own AA guns have fired at our aircraft under conditions where every 14-year old youngster would have recognised friendly aircraft.

I prepare my crew thoroughly for the peculiarities of one-engined flight. Our ground personnel has been informed and awaits our arrival with fire-fighting equipment, rescue team and a doctor in readiness. Everything has been done to receive us. On reaching the vicinity of our base I want to dump my excess fuel but the release mechanism does not function. Never mind, the weather conditions are ideal, nothing can go wrong now. Then, contrary to the accepted practice, I decide not to make a belly landing but let down my undercarriage and come down normally. This takes a bit of time because I have only half the hydraulic pressure, but finally the wheels lock down. After re-checking I bank over the running engine for my landing approach. Aboard the aircraft nobody says a word. I estimate my height while gliding in for the touch-down on the flare path and believe I've got it just right, when I suddenly see that I am a bit too low. I immediately open the throttle, only to realise at the same moment that I have already arrived, and too low! There is a blow against the port wing and we crash onto the ground in complete darkness. The scraping slide along the ground which follows seems endless until at last the Ju 88 comes to a stop with a final jerk. The starboard engine howls up and cannot be stopped – now nothing but out of here! The crew try to jettison the cabin roof, but it is jammed. Next moment there are soldiers outside, smashing the cabin roof away and we tumble outside.

None of us is severely injured, except Theo who is unable to stand up. At the moment of our impact Hans slammed with his elbow into the instrument panel and now cannot move his arm; Hein, our radio man, had his complete equipment thrown into his face and received some flesh wounds, while I had injured my right hand. It could have been worse.

The fire fighters and the doctor are very quickly on the scene. But what happens? This nut of a doctor does not even bother about us, after some of the soldiers told him that none of us is seriously injured: he crawls into the cabin of our crashed Ju 88 and if nothing else mattered, busies himself unscrewing the aircraft clock.*

This is too much for our Hans, particularly as Theo, stretched out on the ground, begins to complain about pains in his groin. When the handsome doctor appears again, Hans calmly walks up to him, removes the clock from his grasp, and then hits him in the face with his good hand with such force that the medicine man slithers over the wing and falls flat on the grass below. That was the last we ever saw of this particular doctor; he was transferred elsewhere double quick.

And so ended another flight to London.

I reproach myself bitterly because this time the accident was my own fault. Why didn't I simply make a belly landing and be done with it?

30 November 1940

We drive out to our crash site, Hans, Hein and myself. Theo had been taken to a hospital and had to remain there.

Our Ju 88 lies on a small field, the only flat and obstacle-free piece of land for miles around. When gliding in to land I had touched a tree with my port wing – that was the first blow we had felt – and then crashed on the ground, hitting it pretty hard. Fortunately the field was longest in the direction we had landed. The machine had come to rest less than 20 metres from a farmhouse and was minus its port engine, which had been ripped out on hitting the ground. We shudder in retrospect, take some photographs, and drive back home again.

5 December 1940

We are sitting in a train to Rheims. At home in our quarters are four signed leave passes for us, but we were asked to do the Staffel a favour and ferry one Ju 88 from Rheims.

It is not exactly very nice, but should not mean more than one day's delay.

---

* A very handsome and accurate 8-day instrument, hence a desired acquisition from crashed aircraft. (Tr.)

...er struggling back from
...gland with its port engine in
...mes, this Ju 88A-5 made a
...od landing at the base
...en the engine bearers
...ally gave way.

...e Stahl crew the morning
...er a dangerous landing on
...November 1940: the
...hor, Hein Hallert and Hans
...ht. The ventral gunner,
...o Goertz, was the only
...w member to require hos-
...l treatment.

6 December 1940

We could have been on leave today but things have taken a different turn. As we arrived back from Rheims yesterday we were told that there was now a total ban on all leave in force. That was all we needed!

And so we sit around with the other crews, waiting for cancellation of the operational readiness ordered for tonight. The weather is so bad that one cannot even think of a night operation. It grows slowly darker outside and, at short intervals, we nervously look up to see what the weather is like.

It is long past midnight when Völling comes into the crew room and announces that tonight's operation has been cancelled.

7 December 1940

In daytime I ferry Unteroffizier Scheller and his crew, one of the newcomers, in a Ju 52/3m to Rheims. He has to collect an operational Ju 88 there and fly it back to our base.

The weather is again quite bad and near Louvain I have to fly so low that I almost touch the trees. I continue flying blind and have to carry out a blind landing at Rheims guided by radio navigation.

Tonight I am again on operational readiness and despite the bad weather I have to fly back to the base right away.

In Gilze we have a repeat performance of the wearisome waiting game of last night. But this time there is an interlude that makes a change: against all common sense we receive orders for an operation against London! The whole Gruppe is scheduled to take off between 0200 and 0300 hrs. This is beyond all reason. The weather is so thick that even our driver loses his way taking us out to the parked aircraft!

Only after we have already strapped ourselves in, someone comes along and tells us that the operation has been cancelled after all. The Luftwaffe has most certainly saved the lives of quite a few aircrews tonight! On the other hand, I would not be surprised if some Party bigwig or Luftwaffe staff officer will now have to wait a day longer for his promotion. We are livid about this idiotic carry-on, and our nerves are all in.*

---

* On the other hand, RAF bomber crews were frequently sent on operations in

Theo has been flown to a hospital in Wismar. Apparently his injuries are more serious than initially thought.

11 December 1940

Another operational flight to London. These attacks lately come under the cover-name '*Fledermaus*' (Bat).

As a replacement for my air gunner Theo I have selected Unteroffizier Knoetsch from the newcomers. He makes a clean-cut and intelligent impression and I feel certain I have made the right choice. The routine up to take-off takes the usual course, and soon we are on the way to the English coast. I appraise the defensive situation some distance from the target area, and take note of the searchlights, AA gunfire and preferential approach lanes for our own aircraft. I then select my own approach course accordingly and arrive over the target almost unmolested at 6,400 metres. I must be among the first because there are no larger fires and only a few bomb-explosions visible underneath us. I glide in with throttled-back engines to be as silent as possible, drop my mines and bank to starboard, setting course for home, still with idling engines. We get very little interference from AA guns and searchlights; their actions are desultory. There is close cloud cover over the British coast near Margate, lit up from below by several searchlights which show up as larger bright spots in the thick cotton wool of clouds. Our tensions ease and Hein switches on some music. It is only then that we notice how cold it really is in the aircraft. The outside temperature is −45°C, with the thermometer right down to its lowest mark.

While quickly losing altitude to get into some warmer air, we suddenly notice a fiery red spot growing visibly larger right ahead of us. At first I am alarmed and look at Hans who is also intently observing the glowing apparition. In the next moment we both realise that it is nothing more than the rising moon, and look at each other and laugh.

---

poor weather and unknown conditions over Germany in 1940-42, before weather reconnaissance, and possibly 3,000 bombers never returned through bad weather and getting lost.

But considering our overheated nerves it is not really surprising that such a normal manifestation as the rising moon should make us lose our composure. Night after night we witness all kinds of similar apparitions in the skies over England that we cannot explain: searchlights that wink or flash in an unusual way, signalling something to the night-fighters or other air defence devices; intermittent lights on the ground; and illuminating flares that are hung in the air above, below and beside us. All these things are sinister to us because we have no idea what they mean and we cannot do anything about them.

12 December 1940

There is an operational order for an attack on London but by late afternoon none of us believes this flight will ever take place. Then the man from the Orderly Room, Völling, appears in the crew room and announces that the operation has been cancelled. We all breathe a sigh of relief; the time is already 2130 hrs.

In the same moment there is the shrill sound of the telephone: Herbert Bohg and I with our crews have to present ourselves at once at the command post. Despite the bad weather we are to fly on operations, just the two of us. It just can't be true! The other crews quietly squeeze past us in the crew room; they almost have a guilty conscience because we now cannot join them in the celebration. Outside we don't even have to get out of the bus: Oberleutnant Stoffregen climbs in and explains the situation on the way to the parked aircraft. They tried everything possible to convince the Air Corps staff, but the powers-that-be insisted that at least a few experienced crews fly operationally, hence us two.

I am the first to taxi out of my dispersal pen. The driving snow is so thick that all I can see is a white wall ahead of me when I switch on my landing searchlight. The cabin glazing is immediately covered and we are blinded. To see anything at all I have to slide open the small side window. We move forward metre by metre along the runway. The snow is at least 20 centimetres thick on the ground, and growing.

I reach the take-off point and stand there with hot-running engines, waiting for the signal. Minute after minute goes by, but nothing happens. In the meantime Herbert too has arrived, as I can

tell by the flashing and extinguishing of his landing searchlight
behind me. Looking ahead, I can just about see two runway
boundary lights, which means visibility is less than 100 metres. The
crew are cursing high and low until I have to order them to shut up.
Then two red flares rise in the air close ahead of us: the operation
has been cancelled!

They really are nothing but damned arseholes! But of course
aircrews have no nerves: they can take anything.

While taxiing back Herbert completely loses his way and has a
proper 'rolling accident'. So that is the complete success of this
operation, a damaged Ju 88! And now the 'guilty' pilot will
probably be reprimanded as well. Should he perhaps have left his
aircraft standing where it was and walked for miles with his crew in
the drifting snow back to his quarters?

13 December 1940

The weather looks like being good tonight and we have to be
prepared for another operation. And that on Friday the 13th! The
weather near base is cloudless, but the return is rather questionable
on account of possible ground fog. We are given Oldenburg as our
alternate airfield.

At 1945 hrs my Ju 88 shoots forward into the dark night sky: we
are once again carrying mines for the Thames.

To get back home as quickly as possible before the expected
ground fog, I fly a flat climbing course at maximum possible speed
and reach our initial point over Margate at 2,000 m altitude. I have
already throttled back the engines in the hope of not being noticed
down there. Visibility is good, and nobody molests us. We glide
towards our target area by compass and stopwatch, hoping not to
run into any ships or barrage balloons. This kind of flying really
strains the nerves, there is no doubt about that. When the estimated
minutes and seconds are up, I drop my two 1,000 kg mines, and
turn towards the sea with both engines at full throttle.

We are back home in record time. There is already a thin fog-like
haze over the base but my landing approach comes off just right.
Due to the haze I cannot switch on my landing searchlight while
coming in to land because it would just blind me, but it does not
matter. I can already see the red lights of the airfield boundary

illuminations, and look forward to feeling my wheels touch the ground, when suddenly the airfield lights are switched off. In the same instant red signal flares shoot up in the air ahead of us – landing prohibition in force!

It is not exactly danger-free to go around again in this situation, but I manage it. Hein badgers our ground control once more for landing permission, but it is refused. Nothing for it now but to make our way to Oldenberg, accompanied by curses from Hans and the rest of the crew.

The initial disappointment over, Hans finds the new course on the map and gives me the necessary compass figures. After a good hour we report ourselves at the Oldenburg flight control office, followed by the other crews at intervals. They are coming directly from 'over there' without having to fly the round trip via Gilze as I did. We had no losses tonight.

At Oldenburg, the preparations for us are first class. At about midnight we partake of an excellent meal served on tables covered with white tablecloths in the dining hall with the personal participation of the airfield commandant. It is a very pleasant way of showing their admiration and appreciation of us and a most enjoyable occasion for us all.

14 December 1940
We are transferred to Marx on the North Sea coast; from there we will be attacking London by night and then returning to Gilze.

I have to fly from Marx direct to Gilze on account of a fault in my compass installation which does not allow me to make night-and bad-weather flights. We land in Gilze at 1545 hrs and for the first time in many weeks can look forward to a peaceful evening and a good night's sleep. Even the sight of Gefreiter Völling cannot upset us today.

Leutnant Hasselbeck crashed on take-off the night before. I can see the wreckage when coming in to land. The crew are all badly injured but alive.

15 December 1940
My machine is still unserviceable. We go for a stroll around Tilburg, the small town not far from our base.

16 December 1940

'Stahl-Bohg' weather again. Exactly as it was only a short while ago: we taxi to the take-off point on the runway, wait there with engines at full throttle and our feet on the brakes, and are then recalled at the last moment. It's normal!

They handle us like stubborn sheep; and then people are surprised when it comes to clashes between the flying crews and the ground officials.

CHAPTER SEVEN

Liverpool and Minelaying

20 December 1940

Today is the last day of the moonlight period: those four weeks of half-moon to full-moon until the other half-moon. This is the period when the operations always get heavier owing to better visibility around the target area. Under these conditions an experienced operational crew, like the few 'old uns' here, would find orientation over enemy territory no more difficult than in broad daylight.

An attack on Liverpool is ordered, and we prepare ourselves during the evening. While Hein Hallert and Heinz Knoetsch look over the equipment, Hans and I sit over maps and plan our routes and times. We are hoping that the wind forecasts are correct, otherwise we have to measure and calculate the wind direction and speed in flight, as often happens. That's not exactly easy at night because it means having light in the cockpit, something we'd rather avoid. For one thing, the night-fighters are becoming noticeably more dangerous, and for another because of the blinding effect on our eyes. It needs only a brief flash of a pocket torch to spoil the pilot's night vision for several minutes. For that reason when night fighters are known to be in the area, I often forgo accurate 'point navigation' for quite some time in favour of keeping a closer watch on the air space around us and the ground. This of course sometimes leads to unspoken differences of opinion between Hans and myself, because he is never satisfied unless he can tell me the exact position, course and time factors in answer to my query at any given minute while airborne. Admittedly, it is probably thanks to this accuracy that we are still alive today, but nevertheless I know when to sacrifice accuracy for security.

We take off at 2040 hrs and I gain height right away. When crossing the Dutch coast we are already at 3,000 metres and still climbing. Our course is to the east coast of Britain, where we have selected Flamborough Head as our check point. If we arrive there according to schedule, we know that the wind-forecasts on which we based our calculations were accurate. Otherwise we can always correct our course by retro calculation and as a result have accurate data for our flight path ahead.

The night is as black as anything because the moon does not rise until much later. The air space around us is quite clear, apart from a few small clouds. We cannot see them of course, but the Ju 88 gives a slight shudder when we fly through one, so we know they are there. While doing so we also develop light icing-up, but that does not bother us.

At 4,000 metres there are only stars above us, otherwise everything is pitch black. The sky 'over there' is cloudless, and we recognise the British coast by the disposition of their searchlights. What follows now is a two-hour flight through almost uninterrupted AA fire. And the fellows down there are shooting well tonight! The dancing flashes of bursting AA shells light up the air so that despite the darkness we can clearly see the small smoke puffs of the explosions. It is worst over the industrial area around Sheffield and Manchester but we get through unscathed.

We recognise our target by the red reflection of fires from a distance of some 80 kilometres. After that, I can devote my whole attention to defensive tactics. On getting closer we are met by the usual sight: fires and flashes of explosions below, and dancing fireworks up in the air at our altitude. The overall situation induces me to make our approach in a wide sweep from the north. We carry enough fuel reserves for about two hours' flying so I can forgo my rashness in favour of safety. My crew on the other hand do not understand this 'loitering', and probably do not have the nerve for it either. Afterwards they are grateful when everything has gone well, but now they are muttering like anything.

I throttle back at 6,000 metres altitude and sneak in over the town. The AA guns are firing at the other end, in the south. This is just right, and fits in with my expectations. The fires below are quite something, and Knoetsch who has never seen anything like it before, is shouting for joy in his ventral gondola. Trouble is, by doing so he also jams our intercom at the most awkward moments.

Hans has an easy task aiming our mines. I fly over the burning port in accordance with his instructions, and we can recognise every detail shown to us on aerial reconnaissance photographs before the raid as if it was daytime. We observe bomb and mine explosions in the port and the town, and then concentrate on our own target. My stopwatch is running, and exactly on the second there are two fiery explosions in our area – our two mines.

Still flying with throttled-back engines I bank quietly south-east and go on our homeward course. All of a sudden everything is quiet around us and the fireworks are left behind. The tension eases, and it is in this state that everything that has just happened is drummed larger than life into our senses. We live through again the minutes after our attack when we came out of the defensive circle and the aircraft was as light as a bird. We enjoy these moments as if experiencing the world for the first time.

I breathe in deeply and relax. Now it's time for my special snack, and I pull out my sandwiches from my knee pocket and eat them with relish. Apparently after my nerves have been strained, my stomach reacts in an especially healthy way: I am hungry!

Another two aircraft are flying some distance to the left of us, and are being heavily shot at. This kind of observation makes it easier for me to avoid the danger zones, especially around Manchester and Sheffield, and pass by at a safe distance.

Finally we can see the searchlight chains and concentrations that mark the English coastline, and start losing altitude. On reaching the East coast I throttle back completely and quietly sneak across without a single AA shot being fired at us.

Underneath us is the North Sea, and the altimeter sinks from 3,000 to 2,000 to 1,000 metres. At long last it becomes warmer in the cabin; we've ripped off the irksome oxygen masks already at 4,000 metres. Accompanied by light music from the radio which is only interrupted when we need another homing fix – we fly back home in a good mood. When the wheels touch down on the runway at 0100 hrs the music is still playing.

On taxying into our dispersal pen, where my chief mechanic Unteroffizier Römhild is already anxiously waiting for us, I switch off the engines and enjoy one second of peace. Then – out. Nothing but to get out of the machine! Once on the ground all five of us shout as one voice: 'Leave!'

This time nothing upsets our expectations, and we are on our way the very next day.

9 January 1941

Three weeks' leave is now behind us. It was great to celebrate Christmas at home, and I was glad not to have to wear a uniform for a short while. On the other hand, three weeks is far too short a time to get back into something like a peacetime routine again. Despite all the joy of home leave and living with my own family I felt a real homesickness for my Staffel and friends there. I kept watching the weather and following the High Command communiqués to have some idea what life in Gilze must be like.

We reported back for duty yesterday, and are on operations again today: aerial mines in the Thames.

Well, that will do to begin with – it is not too far and, if my previous experiences are anything to go by, these flights can be accomplished without any noteworthy interference from the British defences.

When I taxi to the runway the cockpit clock shows 2150 hrs; my take-off time is set for 2202 hrs. There comes the signal: is everything ready back there? And then I am off. With a steady movement of my hand I slowly advance the throttle levers, and our Ju 88 begins to wheel forward. A quick routine glance at the instruments, the dials shimmering faintly all around me – just right. Hans lifts his hand to indicate that everything is in order his side.

The lights along the flare path are flitting faster and faster under the wing. Shortly before reaching the red lamps that indicate the last 200 metres of the runway I pull the control column towards me and we are airborne.

In no time we are past the red boundary lights. This time our Ju 88 sits terribly lazily in the air and makes unpleasant rolling motions due to the turbulent air whipped up by the propellers of the machine in front. Height is the answer, so undercarriage lever 'In' – 'Gear up!' reports Theo – and the electric altimeter begins to show results: 50, 80, 100 metres. Each metre of height has to be literally wrestled from the reluctant Emil! Finally I can retract the flaps; the lever is situated right in front of the port switch panel and I can just about reach it with my fingertips, but all these movements are long since in my blood and I can carry them out blindly, without having to look.

As usual after retracting flaps, the machine immediately gains speed and I have to pull back on the control column to prevent stalling. The airspeed indicator needle moves forward on the scale: 230, 250, 270 km/h. The moon spreads a pale light over the landscape underneath us, and visibility is quite good.

I loosen the harness-belts and make myself more comfortable in my seat. The engines are milling away uniformly; I have synchronised both for harmonious revs. For the time being we are flying at throttled cruising power. There come the flashing light beacons on the ground and these are soon left behind us: YD ahead, YS to port and YW to starboard – we are right on course. These visual signals are quite sufficient to help us check or correct our flight path without recourse to radio direction finding. It is of course a different matter when the weather closes in.

A few more seconds, and the last light signals along the coast are left behind. We are on our way across the Channel to the Thames estuary. After a steady climb to 2,000 metres I throttle back both engines to idling revs and begin our soaring flight to the target area. Visibility is excellent, and it would seem that the British defences have not noticed us. There go the mines! Theo reports that both parachutes have opened, while Hans notes the time and marks the exact spot on his map. Our task is completed.

Still with idling engines, I turn back towards our side and push the throttles forward only after we are just 200 metres over the water surface. But by that time we are already out of reach of the British AA guns.

14 January 1941
Operational readiness! Readiness!! Readiness!!!

It is snowing the whole day long, but we are ordered to be ready. The state of readiness is cancelled only shortly before midnight. Damned idiocy!

15 January 1941

It is full moon tonight, and we are ordered to attack Derby. The sky is cloudless, and the visibility so good that I can recognise details of the English coast as clearly as in daytime. We are flying in at 6,000 metres over The Wash.

Once again it is a flight according to our map and the stopwatch. The time is 2300 hrs when we arrive at our destination. Everything still seems peaceful down there; we are apparently the first aircraft over that area. Right – throttle back the engines to idling revs and look for our target. Ground visibility is very good and the rivers and canals shimmering in the moonlight enable us to navigate visually. There is no AA fire as yet, but lots of searchlights feeling around. This means nightfighters, so let's keep a sharp lookout!

The town is clearly visible, and so is my target, a factory at the south-eastern edge of Derby. Both mines go down – now quickly out of here, and back home.

This time everything goes just right and we are satisfied. Our take-off was at 2205 hrs, landing back at the base at 0120 hrs.

19 January 1941

My 25th operational flight today!

Once again we are laying mines in the Thames estuary, and everything goes almost like a practice trip. We approach 'our channel' at 3,000 metres altitude, throttle back, glide in, drop our mines, glide out again towards the sea, and then set course eastwards for home, flying just over the surface of the water.

I have gained so much practice in the meantime that I can carry out a night landing with the same assurance as a daytime landing.

Take-off 2355 hrs, landing at the base 0140 hrs.

20 January 1941

Today the four of us are decorated with the Iron Cross, 1st class, and the Operational Flight Clasp in Bronze.

Our commanding officer makes the presentation emphatically and solemnly in front of the whole Gruppe which has been 'fallen in' specifically for the ceremony.

27 January 1941

Another operational flight with aerial mines for the Thames.

It is again 'Stahl-Bohg' weather, and we are supposed to fly in daytime. The take-off is set for 1120 hrs, the intention being to find out if it is possible to airdrop mines unnoticed in the Thames in daylight.

I take off with mixed feelings. The cloud base is at just 100 metres and the visibility is zero almost at once. It is not much better over the sea, and so we keep low enough to see the waves and set course towards Margate. It is one of those flights where, apart from the watch and our airspeed indicator, we have no other means to determine our position.

And then the time is up, we should be near the British coast – a dark shadow, and we are already over it. Next moment we are flitting just a few metres over the roofs of Margate. I dare not make any turns in this weather, and simply keep straight ahead. In the meantime the AA gunners have recovered from their surprise and are spinning a thick net of red tracer all around us. I rely on the town being small: we'll soon be out of the reach of the light AA guns. I abstain from pulling into the clouds because that makes finding another 'starting point' an almost impossible task. So we just have to keep at it! West of the town we reach an open field and, keeping just off the ground, I carefully manhandle our machine in a flat turn southwards until I reach the coast again. Hans now navigates us from turn to turn as we bank from side to side and corrects me with movements of his hand. The shadowy silhouette of Margate quickly slips past us on the left, and the light AA guns are again shooting unpleasantly well.

According to my stopwatch we have to fly for exactly 9 minutes 20 secs bearing 300 degrees and then we should be in our target area. Underneath us the grey, smooth sea with clouds almost down to the surface of the water. Anything but a ship now! They have been warned long since of our presence, and raised the barrage balloons and alarmed their AA gun crews.

Suddenly we spot a buoy underneath, then another: our target area, the deepwater channel. Two slight jolts, the mines are falling, and our main task is done.

But we still have two 250 kg bombs aboard for a 'free chase' of shipping targets. The idea is good, but pretty hopeless in these weather conditions. At low altitude I fly eastwards towards the area where the Thames estuary becomes the open sea, hoping rather not to see any ships, than the other way around. It is not only that it would be impossible to make a target-approach flight: under these conditions all the advantages are with the enemy, who can hear us and start shooting at us before we can make a single evasive manoeuvre.

Visibility is so bad that I have to go down to just 40 metres off the surface of the water. And then suddenly it flashes right ahead of us – a grey shadow – a warship! Its superstructure flits past just a few metres beneath us, and we can clearly hear the discharge of many guns of various calibres shooting at us. I get rid of my two bombs and simultaneously bank into the clouds, still followed by the tracer. That was too close for comfort!

And then there is peace and quiet again, and we can breathe more easily. Any hits? There is a gaping hole in the starboard wing, but otherwise nothing seems amiss. The engines are running healthily, and all the instruments are showing their normal readings. That was more than just luck!

The return flight, with some icing-up, and the landing in bad weather back at the base are almost a relaxation compared to what we experienced over the Thames.

4 February 1941
The last seven days have been full of flying and more flying for me. While the other aircrews – when not specifically required for flying duty in this bad weather – stay indoors and pass their time playing some game or sports, or reading or just lazing about, I spent most of my time outside on the airfield, 20 kilometres from our quarters. This kind of activity is not exactly up Hans Fecht's street. He's a passionate Skat* player and can quite easily spend twelve hours and more uninterruptedly bashing cards on the table.

With me it is different. I fly the Ju 88 out of sheer joy, both in good and in bad weather. The pages of my flying log book are filling with entries in addition to operational flights: local test flights,

---

* A popular German card game, especially among the Luftwaffe personnel. (Tr.)

cross-country flights and training flights. I am also using every opportunity to fly mock attacks and drop practice bombs.

By now I have become so well versed on the Ju 88 that I know its limits to the last inch. I can lift it off the ground simply by retracting the undercarriage when the Ju 88 has reached its critical speed. After that I can fly a circle on my starboard wingtip within the airfield perimeter and gain so much speed that I can safely pull the Ju 88 into a steep climb afterwards. At greater heights I try out steep bunts and observe the behaviour of the machine up to its permissible speeds, and beyond. For fun, I also fly slow rolls. I can manage these manoeuvres in such a controlled way that the crew remain seated without fastening their harness belts and no loose objects fly around in the cabin; everything 'stays' in its place.

When all this becomes too much for Hans and Theo, I carry on accompanied by Hein alone. My Staffelkapitän Stoffregen is just as keen on flying and learning more, and allows me a free hand in these activities, as long as I do not infringe flying discipline and order, as they say.

More flying comes my way with the arrival of new crews. All of them are still to a high degree afraid of our Diva from their training school days, and have far too few flying hours on the type to feel at home in it. The way I see it, my first task is to free them of this fear of the Ju 88 and, apart from some hopeless cases, this I succeed as a rule in doing. (Personally I am convinced that at that time there was no aircraft in the world so modern and possessed of such excellent flying characterstics and performance as the Ju 88.)

I am also completely familiar with the technical side of the Ju 88. When not flying, I often pass my time in and around the dispersal pens and hangars, watching and giving a hand to maintenance personnel. In fact, I have already made a name for myself as a universally coveted specialist when it comes to changing a certain spark plug. This particular spark plug is so difficult to get at that the mechanics often have to fumble about for hours before they can change it. By practice, I have acquired a knack of doing this job without much trouble. Of course the others describe it as me having 'midwife fingers' and 'special fingertip feel'. Be that as it may, hardly a day goes by without a leading mechanic coming up to me when I happen to be outside to ask for my assistance.

In the end, with the help of Oberfeldwebel Heiner Mank, our Chief Mechanic managed to invent a specially constructed spanner which considerably eases the task of changing this particular spark plug. We even get a financial bonus for this invention.

5 February 1941

Last night we flew another mining operation, this time to the estuary of the River Humber at the lower end of Hull. We took off at 2030 hrs and were back again after 3 hrs and 20 mins.

The port of Hull has become one of the most important in England, now that London and the Thames are considerably affected by our raids. We come to know that our aerial mining operations have been most successful.

The visibility around the target area is very good and we can clearly see the eight barrage balloons gleaming in the moonlight at about 1,000 metres over Spurn Head. With engines at idling revs we fly over the balloons close above their shining backs and soar towards our target, the waterway. We observe the exact position of the mines and mark it on our map. That's it!

More out of high spirits than anything else I let my engines howl up briefly when we pass the narrow entrance between the Spurn Head and the south bank of the river.

Despite our being hardly 600 metres high, the AA fire I have now drawn is way off the mark. From the operational point of view the most interesting thing is that with our engines at idling revs we are apparently quiet enough not to wake the AA gunners.

The bright moonlight makes our return flight over the North Sea sheer joy.

5 February 1941

I have been given another task again.

They have built a new automatic dive-bombing sight in my 'Cäsar' and I have to try it out. The device is known as BZA (*Bombenziel-Automatik*, Automatic dive-bombing sight).

With our existing dive bombing method we only hit point-targets when the pilot knew certain concrete and exact data, such as the diving angle, diving speed, his altitude over the target, and so on.

Apart from that, he had to have considerable experience on the practice-bombing range and, in the decisive moment, be sufficiently in control of his brain and nerves to carry out his attack calmly and cool-headedly in the face of enemy defences. These demands were just too much for an average pilot.

It is clear that only a few especially gifted pilots have remained consistently successful. Apparently the situation is also very similar among the fighter pilots, where there are a few *Experten* whose score of aerial victories comprises a strikingly high percentage of the total overall.

The BZA consists of an electric-mechanical calculator that acquires the given flight and target data and automatically calculates the necessary values determining the point at which the pilot should release his bombs.

After I had ploughed through the comprehensive technical documents I began to practise in the air, and was soon enthusiastic about this new device. In a series of mock attacks from almost any position and at any given angle I could dive and achieve consistently satisfactory results time and time again.

10 February 1941
Aerial mines in the Humber again. Take-off 2020 hrs, landing back at the base 2310 hrs.

I have to fly Dora because my Cäsar is unserviceable . Everything goes well: good visibility, bright moon, and sleepy AA defences. I lay my 2,000 kg exactly on the metre in the narrow harbour mouth.

I am really pleased that I have been selected, together with other *Experten* from various Geschwader for this special task, on which our command moreover places a high value. If one can navigate to a pin-point accuracy and understands how to manoeuvre at the target, these minelaying operations are relatively harmless. Compared to the modest expenditure the success rate achieved by really 'clean' minelaying is particular high. We know in the meantime the devastating effect of our work. One of the reasons for this is that these dangerous things are not easy to sweep or otherwise render harmless because the mechanism of their magnetic detonators thwarts ordinary minesweeping methods.

My respect for our English enemy is growing more and more.

England has had to endure aerial warfare against a superior opponent for more than six months, and still shows no sign of any weakness. Quite the opposite: the defences are growing stronger week by week. One can now show oneself over England in daytime only in really bad weather, otherwise one is sure to be picked off by Spitfires. The war at sea – or our blockade of ports – is another matter and must have a grave effect on the island.

CHAPTER EIGHT

Zerstörer Crew

14 February 1941

As from yesterday I belong to the select group of *Experten* in every form. We are now carrying out special assignments and are known as a *Zerstörer* ('destroyer') crew. This distinction gives us the freedom to search for our own specially selected targets in the British Isles, but also carries the obligation that we destroy our target. However, all this selectivity does not release us from our part in the normal warfare carried out by our Geschwader.

I select as my first special target the airfield at Linton-upon-Ouse, but my attempt last night failed because of bad weather conditions in the target area. Instead, I dropped my bombs with good effect on the port of Hull. The AA defences were so murderous and accurate that I was forced to terminate my dive at 3,000 metres. Nevertheless, the conflagration left behind in the port confirmed that my bombs had found their mark.

We took off at 2240 hrs, and were back at 0150 hrs.

16 February 1941

Operational flight to Linton-upon-Ouse; take-off 0215 hrs, landing 0540 hrs. It is moonlight, very good visibility, and not a single cloud in the sky – tonight we just must get to there!

We set the course towards Flamborough Head and arrive there very accurately at 5,200 metres altitude. From there on some really precise navigation over land is needed if we are to find our target in a prowling flight without searching around for it too long. We have learned our track literally by heart so that assuming everything goes well we should be able to arrive there without map-reading, despite the fact that the distance to the target is quite considerable.

Visibility is so good we can recognise every brook, every village and even every street. The British AA guns opened up when we crossed the coast, but that was probably more a symbolic greeting, because things were quiet afterwards. I have throttled back the engines and begin to glide, as previously calculated, at exactly 290 km/h and a sinking speed of 2 m/sec bearing due West. Dead on the second we reach our initial point at 3,000 metres altitude, where I have to turn on course 190 degrees and start gliding much steeper. My variometer now shows a sinking speed of 10 m/sec and we all observe intently. The stopwatch is nearing the critical point at which I must be able to see the Ouse. Another five seconds! And there is the big loop of the river, shimmering in the moonlight, which embraces the airfield. I press down even steeper; Hans indicates that he has recognised the target and comments briefly: 'A bit to the right!' – and then I too can see the airfield buildings obliquely underneath in my bombsight. We have built up quite some speed now, and I let go of my bombs which fall across the hangars and buildings. In the next instant I give full throttle and pull our Ju 88 steeply into the moonlit sky.

It is not a moment too soon, because all hell is now let loose behind us down there. But in this bright night sky I can turn and bank almost as if in daylight, and escape without being hit either by the light, medium or heavy AA guns. Theo reports that the whole series of our bombs must have been right on the target, although we could not see any fires immediately after our attack and of course could not wait for developments.

In the event, we manage the 80 kilometres to the coast without being caught by the defences. It is clear proof that one can indeed prolong one's life by doing something in advance, in other words during the flight preparations.

Hein switches on Radio Hilversum for some light entertainment while I cross the North Sea along our old 'oil slick'.

Back at the base, our Staffelkapitän Stoffregen congratulates us especially warmly, and a commendation from the Air Corps arrives by teleprinter the same night.

Hans reckons he would have liked it better if those gentlemen were transferred to the infantry at the front.

16 February 1941

Today they really did well by us: twice to England on the same day! We just managed to enjoy those few hours of sleep after our landing at 0540 hrs before being called to the Operations Room again: armed reconnaissance over the Thames.

We take off at 1840 hrs and set course. Over the target we are shot at by AA guns from every possible and impossible corner, and the weather is so bad we cannot see anything at all. I quickly decide not to take any more risks and drop my bombs on an AA gun position on the southern bank of the river. Even then, it is impossible to observe the results.

18 February 1941

With the 4D + CP to Linton-upon-Ouse again. The weather is so bad we cannot take off before 0410 hrs in the morning. Will I be able to repeat my success of the day before yesterday?

I have no information regarding the weather conditions 'over there' and my secondary task is weather reconnaissance. Cäsar takes us nicely out of the base and we fly in the direction of our well-known Radio Beacon 42 near Amsterdam. I am pleased I don't have to climb higher today because of the bitter cold at higher altitude during these last few weeks.

The flashing light 'YD' slowly passes past us underneath and we have to make a slight correction, 2 degrees to port. Ahead, we can already see the light of the coast we have to fly over, and its sign, 'YW', is the last we can see blinking behind us for quite a while as we set course towards Flamborough Head. We should be there in $1\frac{1}{2}$ hours' time.

It is not at all nice to fly today: the cloud base is just 500 metres and underneath it is very gusty. The sea below is whipped up and the shining phosphorescence of the high-rising wave crests looks quite spooky. It is almost as if one were flying over a badly blacked-out town.

I am wide awake, as always before an attack. My eyes are trying to penetrate the darkness although there can be nothing to see anyway. Occasionally I look over to Hans. He keeps his head upright as if watching the instruments but his eyes are shut. I am sure he is not asleep: it is simply his way of relaxing. It needs only the slightest bump or anything out of ordinary, and he is wide awake. I test this by slightly changing the propeller pitch of one engine which results in a very minor change in the engine noise. Hans looks up immediately and his eyes glance quickly over the instrument panel. His peace of mind is now gone – for a while.

I alternatively envy and grudge him this gift. Life always comes back to him at the right moment, like now: 'Hein, direction finding!', he suddenly says. Hein switches over and with a groan Hans starts getting busy with his direction-finder, quietly but quite distinctly cursing under his breath. He marks something here and there on his map with the minimum use of the pocket torch, then gives a minor course correction and states that we'll be 'there' – meaning Flamborough Head – in fifteen minutes.

The weather gets worse and forces me to go down lower and lower until we are just 200 metres high. Time and again I have to switch on my landing searchlight to see if we are flying in the clouds. And then we are just 100 metres high and I have to decide to go on or to give up.

What shall we do? I still have fuel for more than four hours' flying. Hein suggests we turn around and go back, and Hans mumbles something like 'Nonsense'. However, I am in a really good mood today and turn 160 degrees in the hope of finding better weather further south. The new course leads us at an acute angle towards the English coast and, once there, we'll see what to do next.

I concentrate on my instruments and begin to enjoy this flight. Just 100 metres beneath us I know there is the raging sea, and a few metres over us is the cloud base. These conditions call for 'millimetre work', and that is precisely something that has always fascinated me.

Now we are close to the English coast, indicated by the flashing of individual searchlights. They are fingering around in the clouds, only to switch off again disappointed before passing us over to their neighbours. Every time this happens it seems as if the pale 'dead man's finger' is still lingering on for a while in the dark sky. I can distinctly feel the opposition of my crew, but keep on flying ahead from searchlight to searchlight.

It is a prickly feeling to know that over there, just a few thousand metres further afield, they now have an air raid alarm which in turn activates the whole extensive organisation, just to keep track of us, without any real chance of disturbing us.

Off The Wash the clouds unexpectedly lift, allowing me to climb to an altitude of 2,000 metres. From there we can now recognise the frequently experienced light display on the ground which enables Hans to determine our exact position. Rain hisses against our cabin glazing, and I become worried about possible icing-up.

The night is black, just like 'inside a cow's belly', as we would say. For a while I think of the fellows at home, all asleep now, with the exception of those few I know who will be awake because of us – Römhild, Stoffregen and Schneider. I wonder if Hermann Göring would also think of us, or any of a thousand generals?

It is daybreak when we land back at Gilze at 0830 hrs. The weather over England was so bad that it only just allowed us to carry out an attack on the port of Great Yarmouth. So much for Linton-upon-Ouse.

19 February 1941
We are on the way to 'my' airfield at Linton-upon-Ouse again! It is like the proverbial red rag to me, and my crew have already started grumbling because I won't give it up. They are even threatening not to fly with me any more, but in the end all three of them are ready to go just the same.

Today I have decided to attack by day because 'over there' the sky is supposed to be full of low clouds which will give me the opportunity of quickly disappearing if it becomes necessary.

We are whizzing through scraps of low-flying clouds. It is a messy kind of flying, the wind is bumping our aircraft and whipping the North Sea below us so much it looks as if it is boiling. But good old Cäsar carries us safely through this murkiness as before. Closer to England the clouds begin to lift, and near Flamborough Head we even fly into a completely clear patch of sky. Afterwards, the cloud base is at about 600-800 metres, with 5-6/10 cover. Despite that, I continue on my way hoping that the visibility will not be completely blotted out by cloud cover. The crew is dead against it: Theo and Hein are cursing, while Hans is doing his best to convince me that even if we did get through to the target without losing any feathers we would hardly be able to carry out a proper aimed attack with sufficient safety margin. He is right of course, and I finally give up and turn back towards the sea.

Without uttering another word Hans now gives me the course towards the obvious alternative target, ships in the Humber Estuary. After just five minutes' flight southwards we can see it before us, and there are quite a few ships about. As yet, I have had no experience in attacking ships and keep away at a respectable distance. My intention is to 'let them come', but nothing happens: not a single shot is fired at us. Small boats are busily moving among the 'fatter pots', and nobody takes the slightest bit of notice of us. So this is my alternative target!

With a loudly beating heart I decide to attack, and aim for the nearest large cargo ship, turning towards it from a starboard bank. The peace below is almost uncanny, and my heart seems to be beating right in my throat. If I could I would have stopped there and then and flown backwards, but Cäsar is racing forward. I push the control-stick and go down to just over the water surface. The fat hull of the ship is getting closer and growing bigger at an almost unbelievable speed, and still nothing that looks like defence seems to be moving. I simply cannot bear the suspense any longer and press the bomb release button on my control column, realising almost at once that I will not hit anything because I have not held back long enough. The ship's superstructure flashes past beneath our aircraft while a feeling of shame overcomes me: I have succumbed to fear and failed!

Instinctively I now do everything possible to avoid being hit by the light anti-aircraft guns that have suddenly opened up all over the place. The clouds take me in and offer their protection, but for a while the tracers of pom-poms follow me even there, until finally everything is quiet again.

I start gaining altitude and turn towards home. None of my crew say a word, and the whole situation is somewhat embarrassing. Until Theo speaks up: 'At least we are all still in one piece!', and that breaks the spell. For all of us that's the end of the matter – at least for the time being.

Fortunately during the evening hours we all manage to have a frank discussion about the intricate subject of fear, nerves, ability and the rest. Afterwards we all feel even more united than before, because neither 'side', the pilot nor the crew, has anything to reproach the other with in this respect.

Somehow one episode of the whole affair remains in my mind until sleep takes over that night: if only they had fired on us first!

20 February 1941

My 35th operational flight! Take-off at 1040 hrs, landing at 1400 hrs. The same target as yesterday, and the same weather. Once again I have to turn away shortly before reaching Linton-upon-Ouse – insufficient cloud cover, and once again it is the alternative target, ships in the Humber Estuary. But this time it is different.

The clouds offshore hang right down to the water level, and sleet blots out all visibility ahead. Only the clock and compass can help us to navigate under these conditions. Those few minutes before we reach the target area are not easy for me: the temptation to give up is great. All I have to do is pull into the clouds and explain that nothing could be done in this weather. As for the bombs, I could always drop them into the sea or unload them over some target of opportunity on land. Every human being would have understood my actions, including my three crew members. But: if I go soft now and give in, it will leave a deep crack in my self-confidence and the confidence and trust of my crew in me. My mind is made up: I will remain at low altitude and carry on.

Meanwhile, I swing out eastwards over the sea and begin turning back by guesswork towards the target area where the ships were yesterday. Hans has put aside his map and course-calculator and intently observes ahead, while I can hardly lift my eyes from the instruments. Skimming low over the sea with mushy clouds drifting over the waves demands the utmost concentration and is quite a strain, but we are determined to make it this time. According to Hans, we have just two minutes before we'll be over the ships and then the coast – which we have to avoid at all costs on account of the massed anti-aircraft guns and a thick net of barrage balloons.

Suddenly, on the second, we are right in the middle of the ships; we are flying over them, and Hans reports ships to starboard and some more to port, but it is impossible to attack anything in this poor visibility. All I can do is keep on flying straight in the hope that visibility will improve further ahead. From the left ahead a dark landmass comes into sight, and I immediately turn to starboard. A few seconds later I have more land in sight, but this time straight ahead. I grasp at once what has happened: after flying over the ships we have either by chance, or because of our very carefully calculated flight path, flown unwittingly through the narrow inlet at Spurn Head into the lower course of the Humber and now we are captured like little mice in a trap: I know that all around us are barrage balloons!

Whatever happens, I have to stay over the river. With full throttle I then fly the tightest possible turn to starboard, as tight as I can pull it with my heavily-loaded machine at this low altitude, and just make it: during the last few moments of my reverse bank I spot the dark shadow of the northern shore. As long as I keep this dark strip in sight to my left, I am bound to reach Spurn Head and get out of this trap. After that, everything happens within a few minutes, with Hans helping me by giving directions according to what he can see. There comes the lighthouse on our left, the dark shadow ends, and we are out, thank God!

In the meantime, they have been awakened down below. We are once again over the area populated by all those ships, and tracer comes from all directions. Not that we can do anything about it: we simply cannot see anything in this murk.

I turn north, in the direction where the weather was reasonably clear only a short while ago. True enough, the clouds soon begin to lift to about 100 metres off the surface of the water, and I can breathe more easily – I can even look around a bit now. Hein comes on the intercom and says we should now 'throw away those things' and get out; there is nothing we can do around here. But I will not: the failure of yesterday is simply too deep in my bones.

'Hans, we must try it just once more!' – and he just nods and gives me a new bearing. Once again I fly into the snowy wall, and once again I have to go right down to just over the water.

Suddenly in one spot the clouds lift a bit, and I follow them. At the same moment Hans pokes me in the ribs and points to the right: a ship! And it is already firing at us from all corners.

I attack immediately, flying straight into the red wall of tracer. Cäsar goes down steeply and gains speed, and the fat hull of the ship grows larger in front of me. Next moment I have to pull up to jump over it, and press on the bomb-release button in the same instant. I have a fleeting vision of the ship's superstructure and masts, and the crew crouching behind their weapons, and then everything around us is grey again, stitched through with red tracer. A shout from Theo makes me jump: 'A hit! Look, Peter, right into the middle of the hull!' – Cäsar shoots steeply into the clouds where I pull a tight evasive turn to do something about the anti-aircraft fire. It is not easy in this soup, and I really have to concentrate on the attitude, direction and climbing angle of the aircraft, and so I shout '*Quiet!*' over the intercom – 'Keep your traps shut, or else we'll stall and go in like shit!'

At long last the firing fades and I level off and try to make some sense of my wildly spinning instruments. To complicate matters the aircraft also starts icing up, but then suddenly it is bright overhead and next the sun breaks through the last scraps of cloud. Now we can talk!

'Congratulations, Peter! It must have been at least an 8,000-tonner!' The crew are jubilant. Then Theo comes over the intercom with a more detailed report, telling me exactly what he had observed: two of our bombs fell short, one 500 kg bomb hit the hull square-on amidships, and the fourth fell into the water just behind the ship.

We make our way home happy and proud.

To me, it is like a triple victory: one, by a direct hit on the ship, two, over myself and my fear of yesterday, and three, over my crew. The last is probably the most important, because if there isn't complete mutual trust among the crew of an aircraft all safety in the air is lost.

On reaching Gilze I fly over the field proudly rocking my wings, and then pull an exhilarating climbing roll into the sky before coming in to land.

Now to the official part in the operations room. Oberleutnant Schneider listens carefully and compares our report with a piece of paper in front of him, and then congratulates us on sinking the ship. From somewhere or other he already has another report confirming the sinking by bombing of the cargo ship *Merchant Prince* in the Humber Estuary. The ship was exactly 5,229 BRT* in displacement.

* *Bruttoregistertonnen* = gross registered tons (Tr.)

There is no doubt that it is 'our' ship: the time and and place match each other exactly.

The celebration afterwards defies description. More important than the success is that my own crew of three are again fully on my side, and that I myself am right 'in line' again.

Then there was that quite amazing performance by Hans, who managed to observe things calmly, when there seemed no hope left for us in that Humber mousetrap: on his map he has carefully marked various shipwrecks which were obviously victims of our mines. These shipwrecks probably explain why the inlet could no longer be used, and why many ships had to drop anchor outside in the roadstead.

Our Cäsar has been hit just once, in the port wing, but it is only a small hole ripped open by a light anti-aircraft shell; no vital parts have been damaged. Considering the wild shooting from dozens of ships, including some warships, it was rather a slim achievement by the enemy's defences. Or perhaps it would be better to say that we had more luck than sense?

21 February 1941
We receive congratulations from all sides. Even the 'Old 'un' of 5.Staffel shakes my hand and just about manages to convey his somewhat sour congratulations as well.

Our Commanding Officer Oberstleutnant (Lt-Col) Blödorn arrives from their neighbouring airfield to hear a detailed report. We are not the only ones in the news: Erkens and especially Baumbach have also been successful during the last few days. As a result, our Gruppe is way ahead in operational reputation within the Geschwader.

Over a period of time, a kind of sporty competition has developed between particular formations. The individual pilot would book his achievements and successes for himself and for his Staffel, as well as for his Gruppe and Geschwader. There is also that certain pride in the symbol of one's Geschwader and Gruppe. Our symbol is an eagle diving on his prey with angled-back wings and outstretched talons. The background colour is white, red or yellow, indicating I, II or III Gruppe respectively.

On operational flights we would also carry large silken scarves in the colour of our respective Gruppe, in our case red. For some time past these scarves have given offence to the Army and even our own ground personnel, because there is no dress regulation that would permit such 'extravagance'. In fact these scarves are most important to us: for one thing, they prevent us rubbing our necks sore when we have to sit harnessed in our seats for many hours and can only turn our heads to look left or right. Secondly, these scarves are also intended as signalling flags in case of emergency landings at sea or on land.

Tonight we are once again over London. It is my 36th operational flight; take-off at 2300 hrs, landing at the base 0135 hrs.

The intended target was Swansea on the Bristol Channel but on the way there we are given instructions by radio to attack our secondary target, London, instead.

I must admit we are not displeased about this change in the bad weather: close cloud cover from the ground up to 6,000 metres altitude, with attendant icing and wind of unknown strength and direction. All this would have made an aimed attack on such a small target quite impossible. On the other hand, London is an 'easy one' for us: we have there our well-known navigational aids which gave us a successful release of our mines. Naturally, the British AA guns make our lives sour as usual and force us to turn away several times before we can make our target approach flight, but nevertheless!

Cäsar feels relieved when the mines are gone, and so do we. Pleased and satisfied, we sneak away along our familiar winding pathways, which we could find despite flying blind in the dark clouds. When passing through the critical icing zone we experience loud cracks like machine-gun fire, when chunks of ice fly off the propeller blades and hit the metal skinning of our fuselage, but we are already familiar with that too. Every few moments Hans shines his torch across the wings to report immediately any dangerous increase in icing-up.

I should have got down to lower levels very quickly, despite enemy AA defences but our de-icing system still seems effective enough and I keep on flying.

I finally came out of the clouds just 100 metres off the ground near our base. Below us are the many coloured lights illuminating various obstacles and the rows of lamps along the runways. We are home!

Night landings as such are long since routine and would have been harmless if it had not been for the many beginners who all seemed to want to land at the same time and, in their fearful state of mind and inexperience, often caused dangerous confusion. And so it is this time. Using all kinds of tricks I have to cheat my way in among the many navigation lights of these youngsters whizzing around in the night sky. As a rule my landing approach in such cases is just a quick short 'hook' which is against all air safety regulations. I know that of course, but at least by doing so I avoid the risk of a collision and save myself the eternal banking and turning around the airfield before I can land the 'proper way'.

CHAPTER NINE

Major City Targets

27 February 1941

The weather is so bad that we cannot even think of flying. And that on the day when I had managed to wangle a practice flight – bombing at low level – from Stoffregen.

So we sit around and pass the time, or are simply bored. We are of course on operational readiness 24 hours a day, and that forces us to remain in the crew rooms. The strain this puts on our nerves is almost too much to bear. The messenger from our Operations Room, Gefreiter Völling, does not even dare to show his face any more; I think the nerves of this poor fellow are also near breaking point.

Of course, the gentlemen at the Luftflotte (Air Fleet) have it much easier: they know that we are ready every minute of the day. That kind of situation is greatly reassuring and must make this waiting a rather light-hearted affair, for them. They only have to leave just one soldier at the telephone: 'When something happens, you can find me there or there!' Their's is a comfortable war.

Baumbach and Stoffregen join us at our cloister, 'Mariahof'. They sit down with Willi Erkens and myself in a corner and put on an air of importance and secrecy. Baumbach is by far the most successful bomber pilot, and Stoffregen our admired and respected Staffelkapitän. What are they up to now?

And then they put their cards on the table: the three of us, Baumbach, Willi and I, should cooperate as a team. We should try to obtain permission for special tasks, as specialists against shipping targets. We sit together and plan and weigh up the pros and cons for a long time. Each of us thinks and calculates on the same lines: 'Can

I make something out of this for myself? How high are the risks involved?'

But one of us has different ideas: Stoffregen. He asks me if I would like to be an officer. He is not competent to speak for Willi, because he is from 5.Staffel, but how would I feel about it? Of course I would like to! But there is a problem:

'Sir, I am just a poor old reservist. In this elevated society I have been reminded of that time and again!'

Stoffregen waves his hand: 'Let me worry about that. I just wanted to hear from you how you stand on this point!'

As for Willi, he'll have to talk with his Staffelkapitän, Hauptmann Schulz. Stoffregen then clearly elucidates certain facts that we 'outsiders' have long since noticed ourselves.

'After all, we have three groups of officers. There are those few active officers serving as Staffelkapitäne and Gruppenkommandeure in flying formations and doing all the work. Then there are the very young Leutnante. They come here direct from schools back home, with a training that does not go far enough either fore or aft to ensure their survival. We can see that, night after night, ourselves.

'The third group of officers consists of – well, let us be frank about it – those who only think about their own careers. And these people sit in safe staff seats.

'What is needed is officers who can fly themselves, are serving in the Staffeln, and can ensure that the level of training is raised before the newcomers are committed to operations, as well as seeing that the crews are taken good care of, and not thrown blindly into action without consideration of their actual capabilities for more difficult tasks.'

The whole conversation moves onto a serious note. We has never ceased contemplating the idiocy of war. We state quite openly that it would have never come to a war without Hitler – but we are also agreed that it might have been only a matter of time before our enemies had driven us into a war under other political conditions. We feel strong now, and consider the air war against England as just an interim phase. We can see the effect of our bombing on British towns and ports night after night, and nobody can stop us from believing that this, together with the successes of our U-boats and the psychological stress upon the island people, should soon lead to a successful outcome. Apart from that, time and again one hears rumours about contacts between us and England on the political level to negotiate an end to the war.

We are now discussing quite seriously if it was justified and altogether sensible to carry on aerial warfare the way we were doing.

I can still remember quite clearly our briefing before the first major attack on London. They hung up a very large, about four by six metre, town plan of London in our main messroom and covered it with a curtain. Stoffregen then gave the instructions and briefed us. He was a commander whom I and all the others revered as a model of decency, fairness and soldierly virtues in the best meaning of the word. With a notably halting voice he explained our task:

'The whole town has been divided into a system of target areas. Here you can see the boundary lines marked in red, and the designations of these areas beginning with A.'

He could sense our alarm and our unspoken questions. With slightly trembling lips he went on to explain that, of course, we would only attack such areas that could be described as military targets – in other words, harbour installations, docks, railway stations, bridges over the Thames, and so on. But he also knew that this had not got rid of our apprehension and our doubts, and because of that he did something that no superior of an operational unit would ever do – at least not in the German armed forces. In a prolonged explanation he justified this new tactic, listing the three main arguments for it: 'Reports indicate that war morale on the island has dropped to zero, so that only a few more hard KO blows are needed to end the war. For their part, the British are carrying out regular planned terror attacks on the civilian population in German towns. In a modern war it is hardly possible to determine a clear dividing line between military and non-military targets – after all, by their work the staff of an industrial plant are also carrying out warfare against us, as it were.'

Such explanations made sense, as sheer reprisals will very seldom force an enemy to admit defeat. Generally speaking, the opposite would happen, namely that both sides would lose sight of the accepted standards and the terror would not decrease but increase. Not to mention the questionable military sense of all this.

In the meantime, we have flown a large number of such attacks on

Oberleutnant Stoffregen (centre), Gruppenkommandeur Hauptmann Hinebein (left), and the Zahlmeister (Paymaster) Dannenberg (right) snapped during a lively discussion in the Officer's Mess. Oberleutnant Stoffregen was the author's Staffel commander in 1941 and instrumental in securing his acceptance as an officer. He lost his life in a flying accident late in 1942

Werner Baumbach, one of the most successful Luftwaffe anti-shipping dive bomber pilots, in front of his Ju 88A while serving with KG 30. Together with Oberleutnant Stoffregen he seconded the author's promotion and asked him to join the picked expert Ju 88 crews. On 29 February 1941 Baumbach, Stahl and Arens, another successful KG 30 NCO pilot, were mentioned by name in the German High Command communiqué.

British towns, we have seen Coventry, and experienced similar bombings of London and other towns night after night. Conversely, the number of and effect of enemy bombing raids on German towns are increasing. But we are not punch-drunk and do not drop our bombs indiscriminately into the towns, as has been proved by our aerial reconnaissance photographs. Likewise we acknowledge that our enemy too is making an effort to avoid sheer terror raids, and is attempting to fight in a militarily sensible way (if there is such a thing). Quite often, we even express our admiration for their achievements, and – when it comes to that – their successes: 'Those fellows can really do things!'

The question arises, why don't we take the often easier and less dangerous way out and simply dodge? Nobody can control or keep an eye on us in the pitch-dark night! It cannot be only our soldiers' training and bearing; in this respect our leadership must be living in illusion after illusion. With few exceptions it is our conscience, and our endeavours to be successful, both personally as well as in contributing to the total success. To a very large measure it has also to do with the example set by most of our officers. To my mind the Staffelkapitäne of any Geschwader are the soldiers of our arm who should deserve all the praise our country renders to the Luftwaffe. I don't know of any Luftwaffe general who shouldn't have a bad conscience regarding the Staffelkapitäne and the flying crews, when he puts on his Knight's Cross in the morning. None!

It is long past midnight when, right in the middle of our conversation, we suddenly hear Völling shouting joyfully: 'Operation cancelled – readiness lifted!'

One can almost hear the sigh of relief around the room. Völling remains standing beaming in the doorway, knowing full well the relief and release his announcement means to us. Even so, he has to put up with a remark shouted by someone in the room: 'Arsehole! Take off, and don't show your face here again!' – but Völling is intelligent enough to know that this remark is not intended for him personally, but as an institution.

The mood in the room changes rapidly. Beer and wine bottles appear on all tables as if by magic, and everybody tries to catch up on whatever they were prevented from doing during the past 24 hours. To some it is alcohol, to others a sudden hunger (that is always my reaction), or a hullaballoo, telling jokes, or simply boundless cursing.

I find myself alone with Baumbach in a corner. Erkens has made himself scarce – I am sure he has gone to bed, because he lives completely according to plan. Stoffregen has joined the noisiest and loudest table in the room, although he cannot stand much alcohol: two glasses, and he starts mumbling. But he is happy.

The mood goes completely over the top. Some are howling with laughter at jokes that normally they would have found silly if not tedious. As Willi Hachenberg once said: 'To booze and to fly does one's heart good!' –

One of the newcomers, still a stranger to us all, suddenly appears in the room in his shorts, covered with a sheet around his shoulders. We are all waiting to see what is going to happen. He waves his arms and solemnly announces: 'Oriental sword dance!' and starts to move, minus sword or any accompanying music! Someone giggles, then another, and suddenly we are all laughing till the tears come to our eyes. Silly? Perhaps – but it helps us to unwind.

Then comes the inevitable singer with the usual Volga song, which sobers us up a bit. Baumbach recognises the right moment and stands up, saying that we will continue our talk tomorrow. Suddenly everybody is dog-tired, and the celebration folds as quickly as it had started. Only the dedicated Skat team still remain seated with their cards, while the rest of us go off to our rooms and beds.

It has been quite an evening, and I lie wide awake for some time, while the conversation I had with Stoffregen and Baumbach keeps going through my mind.

28 February 1941

In today's High Command communiqué, we are mentioned by name: Baumbach, Erkens and I! Naturally, we are proud of this high distinction, and feel the whole world is congratulating us. As far as I am concerned, I think that this has removed all reservations connected with my 'unmilitary origin' and low service rank.

Modern as our Luftwaffe is in its technology, it has remained old-fashioned in its spirit. The 'active' servicemen are holding on to their *esprit de corps* that reminds one of the times of Kaiser

Wilhelm II. It is really grotesque to experience how all differences between officer and non-officer – not to mention a reservist – completely disappear in the air, yet immediately after delivering our reports to the command post, when we are still all equally green in the face, the social order of ranks automatically comes into effect again. And not only that: everybody is satisfied with this situation and finds it completely in order!

1 March 1941
The uproar still goes on. A radio vehicle arrives here today and wants us to record a session for the front-line broadcast series. We are driven to the military hospital where Willi Erkens is convalescing from a bullet wound in his hand. All three of us, Willi, Baumbach and myself, then have to endure the usual, in part rather silly questioning, to confirm that we were especially keen derring-do types.

In the evening when exceptionally we are let off duty earlier than usual, we get an opportunity to hear the broadcast in Hotel Rich at Tilburg, where Stoffregen and Baumbach invited me to continue our conversation of yesterday. We were just partaking of pheasant with apple purée, something that does not agree at all with my Swabian stomach, when the front-line broadcast was announced. The dining room was full, mostly with Dutch people of course, and it was their reaction, when the word got around that we were the airmen named in the broadcast, that really delighted us. We were congratulated from all sides and invited to have a glass of something good with them – and that from people who really had every reason not to be well-disposed towards us. It was very much like that time at Le Coulot, when the local Belgian population had showed us in the same way how they differentiated in their behaviour between the enemy power as such, and the individual soldiers who had to fight in the name of that power.

6 March 1941
'Micki' Steinacker has not returned from an operational flight today. And that while attacking 'our' ships in the Humber! Good old Micki; it is a great loss.

We searched for him till our tanks ran dry – nothing. All we can hope now is that he at least got away with his life.

His crew comprised Grahn, Jänig and Herbig, and I was especially proud to call them my friends.

Soon, I will be the only remaining 'old-timer': the others have gone one by one.

7 March 1941

Today is my birthday. I am detailed for an operational flight, to drop aerial mines in the Thames again, but my machine is declared unserviceable by Chief Mechanic Röhmild, moments before take-off.

This reprieve calls for a celebration, and so we drive back home, get out of our flying gear, and proceed to Tilburg – just our crew.

We empty a few bottles at Café Phoenix and talk. The subject of the evening: 'How long can this go on?' Another comrade gone: Hauptmann Schneider, the new Staffelkapitän of 4.Staffel. His last radio message was short and dramatic: 'Engine on fire!'; then silence.

I did not know his crew – none of them.

13 March 1941

The day before yesterday we finally managed to deposit our mines without any noteworthy incidents in the Thames, as intended. And today, on the 13th, it is to be *two* operational flights, no less.

We first take off at 0020 hrs at night to participate in a raid on Liverpool/Birkenhead.

I am dreading that long flight there and back, right across the island. On this operation, we live through a really messy night. In a slow climbing flight I reach the British coast by The Wash, where we are immediately greeted by searchlights. There is not a single AA shot directed at us, only countless searchlights. Despite our high altitude of 6,000, later 7,000 metres, they catch hold of us accurately. It is like flying through an endless tunnel of light. After a while we note furious AA fire to port and starboard coming up from the areas around Nottingham/Derby and Sheffield/Manchester, but apart from this never-before-experienced effort by searchlights, everything is quiet around us. This quiet is really uncanny. I try every trick I know to mislead them down there, but in vain. Every

Liverpool

Hafenverwaltung

Länge (westl. Greenw.): 2° 59' 31''   Breite: 53° 24' 17''
Mißweisung: —12° 21' (Mitte 1940)   Zielhöhe über NN 10 m

Maßstab etwa 1:19 200

Genst. 5. Abt.   Oktober 1940

Karte 1:100 000
GB/E 12

A Luftwaffe target map of the docks at Liverpool.

time I change my direction, the searchlights just follow me. Even the usually effective method of deceiving the defences, by changing the revs of the engines to alter their sound, fails this time. We are captured and delivered! It is obvious we have landed on a strip in the sky reserved for night fighters, those fellows we dread most of all, because their tactics, in contrast to the AA guns, are 'silent' and unseen. In a situation like this, one feels completely offered up without any possibility of defending oneself, either by superior flying skill or the use of one's own armament. Whoever sees the other first* is the winner. We know this only too well, and literally stare our eyes out of our heads.

That we manage to reach our target unscathed probably has less to do with our tactics than with some failure of the effectiveness of the enemy's organisation, or perhaps in their flying performance.

Our predecessors have already done such a good job in the target area that, as so often before, Hans can put away his maps and slide-rule, for the final half-hour of our approach flight. The bright glow on the horizon shows us our way. Thanks to numerous individual fires the miles-long port installations are clearly marked and easily recognisable. Even ships are aflame. It is almost routine now to aim and drop our bombs exactly on our target, especially as the AA guns seem to be too busy elsewhere to bother about us.

We make our return flight always by the shortest way – even though it's through areas where the AA gunfire is most furious. There we know at least what we are up against and can add to our calculations some factors from our own experience on the one hand and leave the rest to chance, or probability if you like, on the other. After a harrowing flight lasting exactly four hours and twenty minutes, the wheels of our Ju 88 rumble once more on the runway at Gilze. It is 0440 hrs. Helped by the labyrinth of lights Cäsar finds

* The Luftwaffe Intelligence were still ignorant of the British airborne radar developments. The first radar-equipped RAF night fighters were hastily modified Bristol Blenheim 1F conversions of day bombers equipped with AI Mk III. Over 30 radar-equipped Blenheim 1Fs were flying by mid-1940. The first recorded success was on the night of 23 July 1940 when a Blenheim 1F on operational trials from Tangmere made radar contact with a small group of Luftwaffe bombers and managed to intercept and shoot down a Do 17Z. No more successes were scored for many months until re-equipment with the faster and much more potent Beaufighter 1F fitted with the more reliable AI Mk IV radar. (Tr.)

its way to the splinter box practically on its own. There, good old Römhild is already waiting for us, and is probably just as relieved as we are that everything has gone well again.

A splendid performance was achieved tonight by Leutnant Hick. Flying exactly the same course as we were, he was intercepted and attacked by a night fighter already over The Wash. One of his engines was shot dead, and Leutnant Hick himself was badly wounded in the left leg. Jettisoning his bombs he managed to dive into the darkness and get away. After that ordeal he piloted his Ju 88 in one-engined flight for three hours at just 400 metres over the North Sea, all the way back to Gilze. Despite his bad wound Leutnant Hick then made a clean belly-landing alongside the main runway. The point is, the entire crew were very young beginners. They must have gone through quite something!

We complete our reports at the command post as quickly as possible. It seems to me that Oberleutnant Schneider who received them has the same weary and green features as the returned crews. A Ju 88 pilot himself, he has been grounded since May 1940 when he was shot down over Holland and lost his left arm. Although he can no longer fly on operations I am sure he has to undergo the same nervous strain as we have. After all, he is the first to receive the operational orders, and knows where we are going before any of us. He is also the one to make out the orders detailing the operational crews, and he also waits for the return of the last crews longer than anybody else, until it is clear that they are not coming back home. And that goes on night after night, with him always conscious that he had a hand in detailing these young crews to face their fate.

We sleep with the good feeling of having been successful and getting away with it once more. Peace and quiet in our cloister is absolutely holy! Nobody gets up until some time in the afternoon, when we shower and go for a meal. And there it is again: another 'operational readiness' for us, the designated target this time being the harbour and town of Hull.

The weather looks good: we can look forward to a regular take-off, without that endless waiting that sometimes lasts long into the morning hours!

It is exactly 2100 hrs when I push the throttle levers forward and move out with the aircraft of our Gruppe. Cäsar gathers speed,

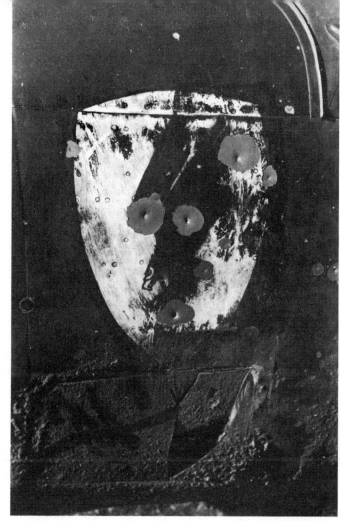

(Left) This close-up of the nose section of a crash-landed Ju 88A at Gilze-Rijen shows extensive damage by British AA shell fragments.

(*Below*) Another Ju 88A that had to crash-land, this time due to battle-damaged hydraulic system.

whizzes past the runway lamps and lifts off, rather reluctant and unwieldy, into the night. The moon is already bright in the sky and its light reflects on the metal of our wings and engine cowlings.

Ahead are the contours of the coastline, and then we are over. Everything is still quiet in the target area. On the way we can recognise every detail on the ground as if it was broad daylight. There is the Humber estuary, Spurn Head, and further west our target, the town of Hull with its harbour.

The searchlights are groping for us again at the coast, but there is no AA fire. They cannot be asleep – so that means night fighters!

And this time they got us. Hein is the first to spot our adversary. As if reporting nothing more than a shooting star we see in hundreds every night, his voice suddenly comes calmly over the intercom: 'Night fighter to port behind!' Without further ado I pull Cäsar into a steep half roll to port and let it fall upside down into the night. Surely, nobody could follow that! I have just levelled off when Hein comes over the intercom again, repeating his warning. The devil! Once more we shoot like a stone into the pitch blackness below. And then a third time! By now we are just 800 metres high, dragging our 2,000 kg of explosives and with a long climb ahead of us to reach a decent altitude for our attack.

While I am laboriously climbing, keeping to seaward all the time, out of range of searchlights and AA guns, I can observe the work of our following comrades at the target. The attack is on: bomb explosions flash upwards on the ground, and the AA fireworks are on full display in the air.

I reckon it will take me at least an hour to reach a reasonably safe altitude for our attack. Who knows what might happen in the meantime? Directly ahead of us is the entrance to the Humber, and so instead of attacking the town as ordered, I decide to drop our mines into the navigable water channel of the river entrance.

Hans switches over the fuses on the mines from land to water use. I am already in a flat turn to port and then level off, gliding silently over the deep water channel. Released from just 400 metres our two 'two thousanders' drop exactly where some fat freighters may make their way tomorrow or perhaps even tonight.

We land back at the base at 2325 hours. This was one '13th' we will remember: we were over there twice in 24 hours.

14 March 1941

The Gruppe participates 'with everything that moves' in a major attack on Glasgow. I cannot join them because Cäsar has insufficient range for this trip: during the last few days it has been modified as an 'illuminator' and has one fuel tank less in the fuselage.

Instead, I am given the task of flying an individual raid on Sheffield together with a newcomer from 5.Staffel, Oberleutnant Flechner.

We take off at 2010 hrs, and are back on the ground again at 2400 hrs. However, what lies between these times makes me seriously wonder how are going to carry out our night raids against the British Isles in the future. It cannot be denied that initially we are quite pleased to be spared that long six-hour flight to and from Glasgow, although we know that the industrial area around Sheffield is thick with AA guns. But things begin to warm up soon after we cross the coast when, as before, the first British night fighters start to stalk us. I even manage to glimpse one twin-engined night fighter, as it crosses my path about 100 metres ahead. Fortunately he is up moon, and cannot see us.

The number of searchlights seems even greater than yesterday, and to increase their effectiveness some of them have been grouped in fives. As a result, our flight path is accurately marked by a pyramid of lights that wanders along with us. Quite frequently our aircraft is hit full-on by a searchlight beam that temporarily blinds me. When it happens, the light beam seems to wander with us for endlessly long moments but then always slips away again. It shows that our matt-painted bomber apparently can no longer be optically traced from the ground in this high altitude. On the other hand, a night fighter should find it easy to follow us for quite a distance under these conditions. He should quickly estimate our speed and course, and determine our altitude as well, if he 'escorts' us long enough.

Fortunately the moon is at an oblique angle behind us. If we were to fly directly into the moon the pursuer would find it quite easy to recognise us against the lighter sky after it had been guided to our vicinity from the ground and by the wandering searchlight beams. These are the lessons learnt from operational experience.

I am trying desperately to think of something that would throw this new defensive tactic into confusion. If only I were not so terribly alone in the sky! Down below, everything now concentrates on me, the poor fish swimming on his lonely way overhead in the night. If there had been several other machines in the vicinity I would have been able to have some idea of the overall situation and react accordingly. Practically every minute somebody asks on the intercom how much longer we have to fly, and Hans patiently answers. The way things are shaping, it is going to be a long night for us!

Finally, the first AA shells burst in the sky and I breathe a sigh of relief – even if it feels as if a thunderstorm has suddenly broken out all around us. Our cabin begins to smell of burnt cordite, but we are already used to that. At least we can do a little something against this warm welcome! Even if we had not known, or our calculations had been wrong, the sudden storm of anti-aircraft fire is the best indication that we are in the immediate vicinity of the target.

Hans crawls forward into the cabin to get a better view. The space below us is quite hazy, but despite that, we can clearly make out the enlarged industrial objective and unload our mines accurately. I fly over the target in a northerly direction, before turning eastwards and for home. In that way I should avoid flying over the same uncomfortable area we crossed on our way in.

Perhaps I've succeeded in irritating the AA gunners down there so much before with my evasive turning dance that they have now abandoned their aimed 'hare-hunt'. They take leave of us with a real barrage of fire thrown up to explode at all possible altitudes. We have never seen anything like it, the barrage is so extensive. This fire-magic dances in the air behind us for quite a while after we have distanced ourselves from the area, and we can see thousands of anti-aircraft gun discharges still flashing on the ground. It is an amazing defensive effort.

This time I am really convinced it was a miracle that we were not hit. After this experience I made up my mind to report at the base that such individual attacks far into the enemy's hinterland and over well-defended areas, are simply no longer feasible. To attempt them will mean the loss of every crew without considerable operational experience. At best, attacks by inexperienced crews will be ineffective.

For a short while everything is quiet and peaceful around us. I am pleased about my light aircraft and the way it now handles. The compass shows our course for home, and I trim Cäsar a bit nose-heavy to gain more speed. The only chance a bomber has to protect itself to some extent from attacks by night fighters is to be as fast as possible, to see the enemy first, and then, either by luck or adept behaviour, to keep on the dark side of the sky away from the enemy.

For these reasons I deliberately select a course so that the moon will remain at a slant to starboard of us. This means an unpleasantly long detour and a longer stay over enemy territory, but it's a better bet. If I had taken the direct course for home I would have had the moon at an acute angle from ahead – exactly what a stalking nightfighter needs to spot me.

A few minutes later Hein comes on the intercom and says that tonight he has really learnt what being 'shit-scared' means. To begin with, there was that sinister approach flight. Then the anti-aircraft fire that was so close our aircraft was really shaken and one could hear the explosions despite the engine noise. And then ...

I interrupt him to remind my crew once more to keep a sharp lookout for enemy night fighters. Apparently my reminder was also a signal to bring life back into the night again: at first individually, and then in ever-increasing numbers as before, the blinding fingers of searchlights start grasping for me. Although this time I am going a good 100 km/h faster the 'light pyramid' follows my Ju 88 just the same! Nothing for it, I just have to dip my nose down to fly faster, even if this means losing precious height.

Time and again now we see green flares in the airspace around us, and it is soon clear that they are also following our course. There is no way of telling what they are, but these signals obviously have something to do with our pursuit.

There is also more life on the ground: individual searchlights start waving their light beams uniformly in all possible directions. I have the impression that they are indicating some flight course or heading. Whatever it is, one thing is certain: my flight direction is being signalled. Apart from that, all kinds of mysterious coloured lights now begin to flash and blink at different rhythms on the ground, and they all mean something.

And then something new: suddenly a string of parachute flares burst into blinding life just to the left of us – exactly at our altitude and very close to our aircraft. I react immediately and bank away to starboard. That is the closest indication of our position in the night sky, and it's easy to see its danger.

From then on I continually and at irregular intervals vary my flight direction, and my engine revs changing their sound. The minutes again seem to drag endlessly until we finally see the coast ahead of us.

By that time my nerves are ready to give up, and without further ado I throttle back the engines to 'noiseless' running and go into an inclined high-speed flight knowing full well that this will bring me into the effective range of light coastal AA batteries. But I don't care any more, and rely on my luck not to fly over areas of massed anti-aircraft fire. There is also my speed: I am now going so fast that apparently all organised pursuit has been thrown into confusion. Nevertheless, quite frequently a searchlight seizes us straightaway and follows, but my high speed prevents it getting more dangerous.

We whizz over the coast at 2,000 metres altitude. A few strings of 'red tomatoes' lose themselves behind us in the dark sky, and then finally we really have peace. I keep my course straight into the dark for a while yet, before I ask Hans for a new compass heading to take us across the North Sea.

As usual, Hein switches on Radio Hilversum for some light entertainment, and ironically they are just playing the submariners' song, 'Wir fahren gegen Enge-land!'

My intended 'other half' Oberleutnant Flechner is already home when I land and report back to Oberleutnant Schneider. He was forced to abandon his sortie after a British night fighter shot up his Ju 88, fortunately without causing any serious damage. It was Flechner's first operational flight, and at first he found flying in a bright moonlit night quite enjoyable. Even the searchlights did not disturb him all that much, he said. But what devilish things were hidden behind their beams he was very soon to find out in no uncertain manner.

Our crew is just as tense and 'all in' as our Glasgow fliers, who land two hours later.

Tired or not, they are filled with enthusiasm about their raid:

once again, a roaring success. Our Gruppe has only one loss that night: Oberfeldwebel Koch. He crashed while coming in to land and the entire crew (Koch, Feldwebel Schwindl, Gefreiter Nikolaus and Leutnant Köppke) were killed outright. It was his first operational flight.

CHAPTER TEN

Promotion

16 March 1941

In the meantime I have been promoted to Feldwebel (sergeant). It's apparently taken a long time for me to be considered as a soldier. The old principle still rules in the Luftwaffe and particularly in our Geschwader, that an airman is a soldier first, and only then an airman. Correctly interpreted and applied, this attitude no doubt has its justification, but unfortunately in my experience the authoritative hierarchy of our Luftwaffe still thinks and acts in the spirit of 'Infantry Regiment No 9, Potsdam' – in other words, as in the Kaiser's days. That we are a highly technical arm of the services and in operations are entirely dependent upon ourselves are facts not willingly recognised. But if what we are doing day after day is not 'soldiering', I don't know what is!

One of our best-known fighter pilots has remarked that fighter pilots should not really wear a uniform but a kind of hunter's apparel*. I would not want to go that far. For my part, although I do not feel particularly comfortable in the uniform, I have grown used to it and inwardly consider myself what is understood to be a soldier in the old German tradition.

Unfortunately with the best will in the world this, and one's achievements as a soldier 'artisan' alone, are not enough to get along. One has to belong to the privileged circle, even in these hard times of war. At the very least, one has to be a professional soldier, an NCO or an officer, to get anywhere.

Since 1 March 1941, my flying tasks permitting, I now have to

* German for fighter or fighter pilot is *Jäger*, lit. 'hunter'. (Tr.)

take my evening meals in the officers' mess. I shall also be an Offiziersanwärter (officer-candidate). For all this I have to thank Stoffregen and Wieting who, as I well know, had to face considerable opposition from other officers to achieve it for me. I also know who my opponents are: the 'traditionalists'! And some who are just envious, like everywhere else.

Anyway, I had many enjoyable hours in our nicely appointed and pleasant mess in a small villa at Tilburg, beginning with the very first evening. I admit freely that I like the elevated environment that reigns there. By this I am not putting down my friends in the Staffel. There too a freer form of manners reigns which is distinctly different from mere 'footslogger' style. How could it be otherwise? The demands upon officers and non-officers are the same, as are the worries, problems and pleasures. So quality and good form are also required to the same degree.

Here in the officers' mess everything is somewhat more polished, but it also can be more hot-headed or more serious than in the crew rooms of the Staffeln. And everything is also less noisy! Naturally a number of groups have formed among the 30 to 35 officers of our Gruppe, according to personal interests, mutual sympathy, or even antipathy. Only in exceptional cases does the difference in rank play a role.

I am very pleased that I am considered as 'one of them' from the very first moment, although I also realise that this has something to do with my considerable experience: I am now one of the *Experten*. But it has also a lot to do with the other officers behaving genuinely and personally towards me in order to make me feel at home in the new surroundings. A civilian would hardly be able to understand what it means in our military hierarchy for a nameless Unteroffizier and a side entrant at that, to be accepted on the sacred plateau of officer rank. Looking at it from that point of view, I am proud – and grateful to Stoffregen and Wieting.

Having secretly feared being treated as an outsider within the Staffel or even my own crew because of these changes, I was pleased to discover that I was mistaken. Quite the opposite: my old friends have remained my friends, and the crew even seems proud to have helped their pilot climb one step up.

Another thing about the officers' mess is that the opposition to the Party*, general among us, is expressed in finer style than on the Staffel level. Thus, whereas in the Staffel the fellows talked quite openly about, say, a *Scheisskreisleiter* (lit. 'Shit District Leader', a denigrating parody of *Kreisleiter*, a Nazi Party District Leader), it would not do here, where everything is weighed up in a different way. How to do it in style was demonstrated by Stoffregen during a minor feast we celebrated one evening. He opened the proceedings strictly according to form by standing up and saying, 'Gentlemen, we drink the first toast to our – rightfully beloved – Führer, and State Chancellor, Adolf Hitler!', and we all stood up and followed the invitation in dead seriousness, knowing full well that with his ironic 'rightly beloved' Stoffregen was expressing his own and our deep aversion.

19 March 1941
The day after tomorrow we are off on leave. Over two whole weeks at home!

The orders for tonight put us on operational readiness: an attack on Hull. The weather does not look all that good. Our briefing is scheduled at 1900 hrs, and brings something new for me and my crew: we are to take off 30 mins before anybody else of our Gruppe and be the first over the target. Cäsar is loaded up with two aerial mines of 1,000 and 500 kg and in additon we are carrying ten flare bombs in the fuselage. With these we are to illuminate the target for the following aircraft until some fires start below. The other crews then cannot miss the target.

This could become quite merry – and of course it would be Hull, that hornets' nest! How we are to operate the flare-bombs is explained to us by our weapons inspector Sievers only just before take-off. We have never seen these things before, never mind dropped them. It is the first experiment of this kind for our Gruppe.†

* Meaning the National Socialist German Workers Party (NSDAP), or Nazi Party. (Tr.)
† The first Luftwaffe 'pathfinder' aircraft were specially-equipped He 111H-3 bombers from KGr, 100 used over Coventry on the night of 14 November 1940. (Tr.)

Exactly at 2100 hrs I push the throttle-levers forward. I have made up my mind that I am not going to do anything amiss at the target; 'Every eye will be on me', as we say. The flight over is nothing out of the ordinary: the usual greeting by searchlights at the coast. After that everything is peace and quiet again in the lonely night. I approach the area where according to our calculations the town must be, from the north, in the hope of recognising the River Humber against the lighter southern sky. The concert of fire from the AA guns begins and shows that we are more or less accurate. Of course, apart from the flashes of AA guns we cannot see anything on the ground – after all, we are the first machine at the target. It follows that we release our first flare bomb more by guesswork than on any accurate observations.

It goes off beneath us but instead of illuminating the ground, it lights up a seemingly thick layer of haze so that apart from some milky whiteness we cannot see anything below us. All we have achieved is to set the AA guns ranging exactly on us, forcing me to fly some sharp evasive turns. During our next approach flight we place our flare bomb quite a bit lower down, and this time we can at least recognise some streets and housing blocks. Hans tries very hard to see more, where the port is, but doesn't succeed.

Nothing for it, turn back and come in once more, dropping our next flare-bomb where we assume the port to be. In this we are guided by our previous flare-bomb which is still burning. Our target area is probably south-east of the first flare-bomb, and there we drop all our remaining flare-bombs at short intervals.

We observe intently: by 'we' I mean Hein and Theo, because Hans and I are fully occupied with the AA guns, which have now started a real target practice shoot with us. Hein and Theo acquaint each other with their observations, but seem to want to make things too accurate for my liking and my nerves. At long last we all agree. The target is lit up, and that's that.

I fly through the furious AA fire away from the target once more, ready to make my final approach and release the mines. The AA guns are now firing at the other end of the town as well, an indication that the machines of our other Staffeln have also arrived. We have done it right on the minute!

We turn back again and carry out a proper aimed attack with our mines. Turning away for home, we can clearly see the fires starting below, the result of our mines and those of the other crews.

Our task is finished.

20 March 1941
Today's High Command communiqué mentions extensive conflagrations in the port of Hull. We are quite proud of ourselves: after all, we were the ones to do all the hard necessary preliminary work.

21 March 1941
Last operational flight before our leave! This time it is another trip to London.

Our suitcases are already packed and we are listening with only one ear during our briefing and final preparations. We pay much more attention to studying the train timetables, to lose the least possible leave time travelling.

The London AA guns fire as usual, and down below it burns murderously. This time it is once more the docks along the Thames. I don't think we have ever seen London like this, we have never before experienced so much fire down below and so much fire up in the air, in the shape of exploding AA shells.

But our mind is on other things. We think about our forthcoming leave on the way out and still in between the flashing shell explosions around us and in sight of all those conflagrations on the ground. And then we think aloud and talk about it: can we manage to catch the earliest possible leave train tomorrow morning?

Our job for tonight is done. The peaceful night on the way home over the sea seems the best prelude there could be to the well-deserved two and a half week rest that lies ahead of us.

7 April 1941
We arrived back from our leave yesterday.

Apart from purely personal matters that concerned only my wife and myself, or our family, I feel as if I've been in a different world. Certainly, it was flattering to be celebrated as a 'hero', as 'one of our England-flyers' who are paying them back in their own coin 'over there', and as one who had even been 'on the radio'. Yes, those two weeks were wonderful. But now somehow I am glad to be back again in the Staffel.

When I report back, Stoffregen thinks that I have not missed much. The Gruppe has used the period of darkness to prepare for the full moon, which begins today. I seem to be right on time.

My next visit is to my Cäsar and its trusty caretaker, Römhild. He assures me he has protected our trusty kite from all misuse. Whoever wanted to take Cäsar in the air had to give up their plans, because Römhild always found some technical or other reason to declare the machine unserviceable! And so Cäsar is ready and waiting for us.

To get used to it again, we make an extended practice flight the same morning, before our midday meal. It is a beautiful day, the sun is bright in the sky, and a peaceful landscape stretches out beneath us. With the whole crew I enjoy the regained adventure of flying. I demand everything, the utmost Cäsar can give: I let it climb vertically into the sky and wait to see to which side it would want to stall out, then shoot vertically downwards, racing for the ground. I believe all four of us enjoyed this game in the same measure. We might as well: tonight we can expect the hard reality of war again anyhow.

The nerve mill begins to churn in the usual way shortly after our midday meal. We are ordered to be in operational readiness for tonight, although the target and the times are not yet known, as usual. The hours crawl by in the tormenting suspense we have experienced a hundred times before. It is a good thing that I managed a really good 'training session' this forenoon! At least the weather looks good.

Völling finally appears at 1715 hrs and lets it be known that briefing will be at 1800 hrs. 'Let's hope they chase us into the Thames today,' says Theo, 'that'll be just right to get us accustomed to things again!'

Somehow I have an idiotic fear of tonight. To calm myself down, I repeatedly remind myself that there is no one else here as experienced as myself. And that all this time the Tommy 'over there' has always been just that little bit sillier than me. So why should it be different tonight? As long as the engines remain healthy, nothing can happen to us!

At our briefing, Stoffregen himself arrives in person and explains our operational task. The target for tonight, to start the new moon period, is Greenock, an important naval port at the western exit of the Clyde in Scotland. Then follows the list of detailed crews: 'Feldwebel Stahl will fly Dora because his own Cäsar with its special equipment is not suitable for this long trip.' The estimated flying time is about six hours, quite a long stretch.

We make our preflight preparations with accustomed care. Together with Hans, I work out the navigation calculations while Hein looks after his radio bits. Theo takes care of our provisions and checks the emergency and safety devices for all of us. With foresight and care, he has also organised himself a pneumatic cushion for the long flight.

In a somewhat indifferent mood I strap myself into my parachute and my seat. As usual, Hans takes ages to force his tall frame up the small ladder and through the entry hatch. He always dawdles that long, apparently to have another reason to curse about 'those idiotic people who built such an aircraft.'

Hein on the other hand sings his usual 'A man must travel time and again …' and sets my nerves on edge for the n-th time. He is in the habit of singing that inane 'hit tune' every time we climb into our aircraft, then again just before we take off, and once more when we are airborne. Phew! Only Theo is a stoic.

I myself feel simply 'itchy' and irritable. Everything seems to move far too slowly for my liking! Really we are all equally oversensitive and nervous and each one of us reacts according to his temperament.

'Theo, press in those safety buttons at last!'

'It is always the same damned dawdling till all you Heinis finally manage to get into the kite!'

It is always the same. I have to put on an act every time, before I can start the engines.

At long last! The control lamps light up, the instruments begin to register. 'Port free!' The starter hums after I have pressed in the lever. Clutch in – the propeller turns over with a jerk. Red flames shoot out from the exhausts, and then the 1,200 horses begin to move somewhat reluctantly. 'Starboard free!' The starboard engine too begins to spit, and then to run evenly. I give full throttle successively port and starboard to check the ignition and generators. Then in turn I check the oil pressure, oil- and coolant temperatures, boost pressure, fuel pressure, hydraulic pressure, as well as the fuel and oil supply. Everything is in order – away with the wheel chocks!

We roll out into the night to our take-off position. The searchlight briefly lights up our ground chief Römhild waving his cap. The moon is already up over the eastern horizon, a narrow sickle. Its light is still far too weak to be of any use.

It is 2035 hrs when I taxi across the airfield towards the green lamps that indicate the beginning of the take-off runway. Just then the navigation lights of my predecessor whizz along the flarepath, and I can follow right away. I am determined to use every metre of the take-off runway and park Dora way behind the first green lamp. I check everything once more, then: Lock the tailwheel; flaps out 25 degrees; trim to 'normal' – all clear?

'Let's go!' I call out, and the customary reply comes back from the crew as always: 'Let's go!' For me it is the signal that everything is really in order on board. I slowly advance the throttle levers right to the stop and then let go of the brakes. Sparks shoot out of the exhaust stubs and the engines roar out. Dora begins to move forward with a powerful jerk. Hans lifts his left hand to indicate that 'everything reads right' and that the engines are running the way they should. The white lamps of the flare path are already whizzing past under the port wing. The instruments in front and all around me show their phosphorescent dials, but I leave their reading to Hans. Right now I must concentrate on holding Dora straight, and judge the right moment by the pressure on the controls when to lift the tail to gain more speed and become airborne.

Our take-off runway is 1,400 metres long. It may seem a lot but is not all that much when one speeds along there at 200 to 220 km/h. The red lamps of the final 200 metres come nearer. Steady, I wind the trimming wheel to 'tail heavy' with my left hand and simultaneously pull the control column with some force towards me. My trusty kite now wants to be free and away, makes a slight jump, and leaves the ground.

The red lamps of the boundary lighting skim past us just a few metres below. We cannot call this flying yet, the Ju 88 is 'swimming' ponderously through the propeller turbulence of the machine in front, now somewhere ahead of us in the dark.

I retract the undercarriage. I have to stretch right forward with my left hand as far as I can to reach the lever, but I am used to that now. 'Wheels coming up!' calls out Theo. The strain does not ease until the altimeter is registering 100 metres. Now is the time to retract the flaps; the machine always seems to sink a bit but gains in speed and then really begins to fly. I help her along by trimming and pulling on the control column. It is only now that I can throttle back the engines a bit and with the help of the altered propeller-pitch, change over to cruising power.

We are flying into the night. It is dark all around us, with no lights of any kind near or far. Only the stars twinkling high above us and the dull glow of the instrument dials in our cabin are points we can fix our eyes on. Carrying 1,500 kg bombs and 3,600 litres fuel, our kite is loaded to the limit of what it can take. We get on our course, in a flat climb, and the well-known flashing beacons come in sight and are then left behind. We sense more than see the coastline, and then the compass shows our course to Greenock.

Groaning, Hans bends towards the direction finder: 'Hein, take bearings!' Our radio man switches the medium wave receiver to direction-finding, so that Hans can pick the right radio station to determine our base line. There follows a confusion of squeaking radio signals from various stations till Hans has found the right frequency. The measured compass bearing of the radio beacon behind us gives him our baseline which he draws on the map and then finds a deviation. This means that the wind forecasts were wrong, or the wind has changed in the meantime. As usual, independently of each other we both work out the necessary correction: 120 seconds to 30 degrees starboard, then set course, correction 6 degrees.

In the meantime we have climbed to 3,200 metres. I decide to remain at this height because the engines are running at their most economical here, giving us optimum performance/fuel consumption ratio.

Time and again I glance at the watch: we should be at the target in 1 hour 50 mins. Beneath us we can make out an unbroken cloud cover although according to our weather forecasters it should break up over the British mainland.

Across to port there is AA fire – that must be Hull. A bit further north searchlights are drawing white spots in the clouds; that'll be Newcastle. Sometimes it is a good thing that there are AA guns, it always makes it easier for us to navigate over enemy, and our own territory, for that matter.

We fly over the eastern coast of Britain still in unbroken cloud cover, and the countless searchlights indicate that we have reached land. Why are there so many searchlights: could it be to assist their night fighters again?

Far ahead we can see a real fire-dance of AA explosions in the sky. That must be the target area, because otherwise there is nothing much in this northern part of the British Isles. I begin a steady climbing flight, keeping towards the AA fire. Our Ju 88 has just reached an altitude of 4,200 metres when we reach the fireworks. The AA gunfire is well laid, as we can judge from the explosions flashing uncomfortably close to our Dora. The cloud cover beneath us is still unbroken, lit up by searchlights from underneath. This creates an effect of flying over a giant pane of frosted glass. Hans carries out another reverse calculation on his slide rule and confirms that we are definitely over Greenock.

I have no choice: I just have to drop my bombs blind. I leave the fireworks once more to try and determine the approximate middle of the witch's cauldron, and then fly towards it and let my explosives fall. Two jerks of the aircraft confirm that we are rid of our load. Bon voyage!

A steep turn of 180 degrees in the middle of the fireworks brings us on the course for home.

Soon we are enveloped in peace and quiet over the Scottish Highlands again. A short while later we are again given navigational assistance by the searchlights and AA fire of Newcastle and Hull, and then it is all dark underneath us: the North Sea.

Unexpectedly, the clouds below begin to break up and our timing tells us we can expect to see the Dutch coast at any moment. A light beacon flashes ahead of us, and we are relieved to see that it is 'YW'. Just twenty minutes later we are over the lights of our base. Once more, we manage to get through the confusion created by our dear beginners during their landing approaches, touch down in one piece and quickly taxi our Dora to her shelter.

And then nothing but out! Tonight we have struggled through almost 2,000 kilometres in the air, to be shot at and finally drop our ammunition blind into the clouds. Talk about cramps!

While we are straightening our bones again the crew let fly with some choice curses aimed at 'those up there', and especially the 'weather frogs'. I can only add that it is the dear God who makes the weather and not the weather frogs, but it is a small consolation after our long trip over the clouds.

10 April 1941
Operational flight with 4D + CP to Newcastle.

Today, I have to relinquish Theo. In his place I have been detailed to take Unteroffizier Weidemeier, a mechanic from our ground personnel. These measures are intended to avoid estrangement between the flying crew and ground personnel, and also to give the technicians at least a superficial impression of our operational activities. After all, that is what they are working for, sometimes without getting any perceptible recognition for their efforts.

I think it is a good idea, because generally speaking the chaps are good sorts and are doing a lot for us. On the other hand, a foreign body aboard also means a considerable drawback within a well played-in crew, and for that reason only 'easier' operations are selected for this purpose, flown by our older and more experienced crews.

This problem of estrangement between the permanent ground personnel and the flying crews of the Staffeln has come about simply because the continuous losses have been so high that the younger crews were hardly long enough in their formations to become friendly and known to them. An additional factor is the steadily worsening training of flying crews, which in turn is having an adverse effect on the work of the ground personnel, because an increasing number of senseless complaints and hold-ups are either reported or caused.

Soon the young, inexperienced and still strange new pilot is no longer taken seriously by the old and cunning ground crew technicians. For these reasons, and in the interest of the sympathetic

Weidemeier I hope that things will work out 'nice and orderly' tonight.

Our outward flight over the sea does not create any problems. The sky is noticeably lighter than the night before, and only scattered cloud formations are floating beneath us. Having taken off only at 0025 hrs, we can see the fires in the target area a long way off: the crews preceding us have made sure the target is well and truly marked some time before our arrival.

Tonight we are carrying a mixed load consisting of one multi-bomb container with 1,000 incendiaries and two HE bombs of 500 kg each.

Ground visibility at the target is very good on account of the moonlight and several large conflagrations. Coming in at 4,000 metres altitude, I approach with throttled-back engines in a wide spiral from the west for better orientation and to be able to continue homewards right after the attack. Of course, my bombing run is also measured according to the AA fire, which just now is particularly busy at the other end of the target area.

Weidemeier, to whom I have given instructions to keep strict silence, apart from in exceptional circumstances, breaks out in enthusiastic jubilation at the sight of the fireworks below. We were just like that once, but have long since overcome this feeling. I let him have his enjoyment, but take extra care for our safety by appraising the situation in the sky around us and on the ground. Fortunately tonight's performance is relatively harmless compared to what we have experienced before. We are even able to observe the explosions of our bombs before being caught by some well-directed AA fire on the way out. A steep turn obliquely downwards saves us from further trouble.

On our flight back home over the peaceful dark sea we are all pleased for Weidemeier who has now seen something of what our operations are like. It was all there, in measured doses so to speak: some clouds and some clear night sky, a bit of moon, some AA fire and searchlights, and some fires and explosions on the ground. In short, an attack that was right according to the book.

In contrast to this blooding of the ground crews, there is a distinct aversion among the old hands to taking along war reporters or, even worse, General Staff officers from our superior staffs. To us, they are nothing more than 'sandbags'; in other words, we just have to drag their weight with us. In addition to that they are also a danger to us, simply because they cannot carry out any functions on board the aircraft. Apart from that, they're usually frightened out of their wits!

The other thing we will not put up with is that we, the old hands, are being used merely to help them graduate in the 'Iron Cross, 2nd Class, course of instruction' with the greatest possible safety, and – apparently just as important – ensure that they will qualify for their additional flying pay and provisions for another year.

11 April 1941
Today's good flying weather again points to an operation at night. Accordingly, the usual mood starts pervading the billets already early on. Theo has characterised it as 'tormented humid outspokenness'.

With this kind of mood around, my chief concern is always the aircraft. On these long-range flights at night under unknown weather conditions and with insufficient navigational aids, mainly over enemy territory, it needs only one small item to go wrong to result in a disaster. For that reason my ground crew chief and myself are at one, heart and soul. We handle our kite as probably no other technical object has ever been handled; we know every screw and bolt, every hydraulic pipe line, and no unusual sound in an engine escapes us. There are times when I stroke the cold metal skin and feel almost a tenderness towards the splendid aircraft.

In the afternoon I have to fly with Hans in a Bf 108B Taifun to Soesterberg to collect some spare parts. It is one of those small joys that comes my way because of my special standing as an 'all-weather pilot'. The 140 kilometres flight there and back is sheer pleasure with the small birdie.

There is the usual operational readiness in the evening. Everything remains uncertain until long past midnight when we are finally informed there'll be no operations tonight. No reason is given for the long delay. Relieved, we leave the crew room and tumble into our beds.

15 April 1941

I take off at 1055 hrs in the forenoon with the seemingly eternally sick Dora for a local test flight. The idea is to check out the port engine and I am accompanied by Hein and an engineer from Junkers.

It is an April day that is as beautiful as it is rare. The sky is decorated with 5/10 cumulus clouds piled up in a splendid formation – a fine sight to behold. All this makes me feel carefree and even cocky. We test the engine while still climbing and that really completes our programme. But the beautiful weather and the peaceful flying in broad daylight simply keep me up in the sky. In short, I let off steam and romp around in the sky so much that finally even Hein has enough and asks me to land. While I have this chance I fly the Ju 88 in between the towering white walls of the clouds not only as if there was no 'up' and 'down' but pulling it as well into controlled horizontal and climbing rolls. Once again, the Ju 88 proves itself in great style, despite its 12 tons.

I approach the base in a steep inclined flight out of a high turn to roar across the airfield at low altitude, and then pull into the sky in a climbing roll. It is a fitting climax to a great time in the air!

This finale was witnessed by Stoffregen who first tries to play the strict superior, but then pulls me aside to ask in detail how one goes about doing it!

In the evening, the inevitable operational readiness followed by orders to attack Newcastle. We are already taxying out to our take-off place in complete silence aboard when Hein suddenly reports a fault in his wireless equipment and I have to turn back. After a check it is evident that this fault cannot be rectified quickly, and we have to remain at home.

All this is more than a bit annoying because by the time one is standing ready to take off, the worst is already over: the inevitable attack of faint-heartedness has been overcome.

CHAPTER ELEVEN

Raids on the Ports Continue

17/18 April 1940
Operational flight to Portsmouth. Take-off at 2155, landing back at 0145 hrs.

Tonight's problems are more of the flying than military kind. The outward and return flights are mainly over our own, occupied territory. On the way out we fly south-west almost to Cherbourg, before making that relatively short hop of about half an hour across the Channel, and we are at the target without having had to fly over enemy territory.

It is quite a bright moonlit night and our outward flight goes smoothly, helped along by numerous clear ground navigational aids in our own territory. Our way to the target is shown quite a distance away by a fiery glare and AA fireworks in the sky. The town and port of Portsmouth are covered by 3-4/10 cloud, in addition to a mighty smoke cloud fed by fires down below. All this greatly reduces ground visibility in the target area and I am hard put to find my way between the big dummy conflagrations and the real fires. To make things worse, we are also caught by AA guns in no uncertain manner. It is so bad that Cäsar does not just make the odd hop and skip as it does when some shells go off rather close but literally jolts through the waves of detonations. Some of the explosions are so close we can see glowing splinters shooting in all directions. And there does not seem to be any end to this cannonade! No matter how I twist and turn, the AA guns follow me!

Despite this I manage to place my bombs on the target after we had pulled aside for a while and then made a quick bombing run using an unguarded moment. It was a close thing, but still Cäsar remained unscathed. The only damage is one splinter that has punched through the ventral gondola and remained stuck in Theo's fur-lined boot, just scratching the skin of his calf. This is what we call being in luck!

On the return flight over France, while we are steadily rumbling along on our prescribed route home, relieved and half dozing, we are suddenly shot at by our own heavy and light AA guns. We are exactly at the correct altitude of 1,000 metres, and the AA gunners must know that at this altitude and time, and along this course, there will be our own aircraft on the way back from England. So why are they shooting at us? Hans quickly loads his flare pistol and fires the recognition colours of the day – no effect! He loads and fires again, while I am forced to fly evasive manoeuvres. Instead of abating, the firing is actually increasing, and we do not have peace until I have rammed the throttles full forward and dived out of the area at top speed.

How and why do such errors happen time and again? I personally know of a number of comrades who have been shot at, wounded, and even shot down by our own AA guns. More than that: I once witnessed a truly blatant and tragic case myself where a badly shot-up Ju 88 was returning home on one engine in broad daylight. As it levelled off to prepare for a belly landing on the runway, and we all breathed a sigh of relief for the crew because the worst was now over, the Ju 88 was shot down by our own light AA guns in front of our eyes!

19 April 1941
I take off for Germany with a Ju 52/3m, and I am supposed to be back in the evening.

After a stop-over at Perleberg – a grand welcome there – I fly on to Parow near Stralsund and land in the worst imaginable weather. It is so bad the airfield flight control forbids me to fly back again. We are not unhappy about spending a night in peace for a change, but it is not to be: a teleprinter message from Stoffregen soon afterwards orders us to return at once 'for operational reasons'. That of course changes the opinion of the Hauptmann in charge of flight control at Parow and I become a kind of 'honorary release' to fly back despite the bad weather.

Damn it all! We are in a stinking bad mood as we climb aboard our Ju 52 again. The cloud base is just 50 metres when I take off, jolted by gusty winds. The Ju 52 leaves the ground reluctantly and for a while I remain at low altitude before pulling up into the clouds.

We land dead-beat in Gilze at 1900 hrs, and hardly have time for a meal, before having to prepare for a night operation. This time it is a major effort against London by all bomber formations. According to plan, all units are to attack London with maximum possible strength twice and, if at all possible three times tonight.

The vast majority of crews consist of green beginners and I can only hope that things will work out all right during the first landing and after the second take-off. On those occasions there is always so much danger to my mind that it almost equals whatever the British defences have prepared for us. The regular crashes that take place when coming in to land at night are a clear proof of this.

The pre-flight preparations on the ground are perfect. The first machine is scheduled to take off at 2100 hrs, followed by the others at two-minute intervals. I am one of the last, and push my throttle levers forward at exactly 2145 hrs.

It is not an easy take-off on account of some cross-wind. After all, I am dragging along my 2,000 kg of bombs as well! After crossing the coast a loose cloud cover pushes itself in between us and the sea which now looks black and sinister through the gaps in the cloud. Despite that, the visibility is excellent and we can see the flashes of bombs dropped by our predecessors already 200 km from the target. We forego all navigational calculations: it is quite sufficient just to keep flying in the direction of the fireworks.

We are in a relaxed mood because the weather looks fine and under these conditions London normally does not create any difficulties for us any more. Hein calculates there must be at least 500 aircraft operational, and that would mean anything between 800 and 1,000 bombers over London tonight!

The British AA guns greet us already at the coast, probably near Harwich, but we soon have our peace again. Left, right, ahead and behind fly the machines of our comrades – how can the enemy effectively concentrate his defences under such conditions?

We manage to reach the target area without any dangerous harassment apart from the scrambling of hundreds of searchlights. The usual picture unfolds before our eyes underneath: widespread conflagrations, flashes of AA gunfire, and the unmistakable burning from bomb explosions.

We recognise the bends in the Thames while I am looking for the release point for our 'one-tonners'. We can also clearly see large numbers of barrage balloons against the glowing background, but we keep way above them.

As soon as the bombs are gone we turn homewards, but it takes quite a while before it is quiet down below and the peaceful night embraces us again. If London has such a terrible time now, what will it be like after the second raid? One cannot bear to think about it.

With music in our ears, courtesy of Radio Hilversum, we return back home again. We have to be extra careful around the base tonight because of the many excited and fumbling beginners, but somehow everything goes smoothly while I circle the field at safe altitude. Aircraft after aircraft come in to land and then taxi away, and I manage to squeeze myself into a gap. Within moments we are flattening out, touching down, and taxying away. A flashing green light indicates my parking place where Cäsar will be refuelled and bombed up again.

I have hardly switched off the engines when a fuel bowser drives up in front of the machine. So much for a break! We climb down and are immediately driven to the Operations Room. Everything seems to be topsy-turvy here, everybody is in a great hurry, and all have an awful lot to report.

We have exactly one hour before the second take-off, including our pre-flight preparations.

When we are finally driven out to Cäsar again, Römhild comes to meet us despondently and reports that our machine is unserviceable. Apparently an AA shell splinter has ripped a hole in the starboard wing and it could mean some serious damage. I reply quite honestly that I don't mind at all. It is only now, when the strain is easing a bit, that we realise how dog-tired we really are. After all, within the last twelve hours we have been in the air for at least nine not exactly easy hours considering the weather and operational conditions.

We let ourselves be driven back to our billets again where, tired as we are, we do not retire to our beds but await the return of the other crews. Their reports are enthusiastic about the successful outcome of the second raid, and everybody is very pleased. Only two crews are missing, but they were not known to us.

22 April 1941
The forenoon today was spent in abundant practice flights. I whirled in the air, demanding the utmost of the machine and my own flying skill. Although my crew sometimes think I am going round the twist they know different, that these twists have already paid off in the end.

The night sees another attack on England. For me, it is a mining in the Bristol Channel, but the target area is completely hidden by unbroken cloud cover stretching almost down to the ground. As under these conditions it is not possible to carry out an aimed mining operation we turn southwards, where we can see a large fire on the ground. It is Plymouth, and I am sure it is more sensible to unload our mines there.

24 April 1941
Once again we are in the air carrying 2,000 kg of mines. Our target for tonight is again the Humber. There is hardly anything new in this for us: the Humber estuary will soon be like our second home.

Shortly before reaching the target, as we can already see the familiar tongue of Spurn Head and the numerous barrage balloons over it in the light of the half moon, we suddenly spot an enemy night fighter right close to us, flying almost parallel to our own course. Apparently he cannot see us because we are on the dark side. Nevertheless, a moment later my Ju 88 is half on its back disappearing into the black darkness below. A short while later our mines splash in, right on the intended spot, into the deep water channel.

We have been airborne for three hours and ten minutes when the wheels of our Ju 88 are once again rumbling along the runway at Gilze at 0115 hrs.

26 April 1941
Last night we were saved from an operational flight, but had to wait until long after midnight before the sortie was finally cancelled. We

had no idea of the intended target.

For all that, we are once again on our way to Liverpool tonight. To my mind, that town is the worst the Island has to offer, perhaps because I always have some nasty experiences while flying there. They have again selected a special dainty morsel for me: in addition to our 500 kg LM-A and 1,000 kg LM-B aerial mines, our Ju 88 is also carrying ten flare-bombs in the fuselage. I am supposed to play the role of an illuminator and 'firelighter'!

During our briefing Stoffregen named us in fun the UFA crew*, but that is the kind of fun I would gladly forgo.

Flying over an unbroken cloud cover and just fifteen minutes before reaching the target area we are ordered by radio to turn back and attack the alternative target, Hull.

'Well, look at that! They can even think!' comments Hans. It does not happen very often.

Relieved, I turn around. Hull is not difficult to find because the whole area is abundantly marked by searchlights and AA fire. I let go of my first flare bomb which illuminates a partly broken cloud cover beneath us and calls forth increased exertions on the part of the AA guns, although their fire is not very accurate. But that is all: we cannot see anything. I turn around and approach the area several times, hanging my parachute lanterns in the gaps between the clouds below in an attempt to recognise something that would justify us carrying out an aimed bombing run, but in vain. In the end I just have to give up and fly northwards in the hope of finding better visibility.

Over Middlesborough we can finally orientate ourselves beyond question, and I make my bombing run on the town using our old proven tactics. The AA defences are only moderate so that we can drop our explosive load quite accurately. On the way out, Hein and Theo report the flaring up of a fire. Perhaps it has paid off after all for us to fly around for hours on end in the dangerous night skies over England.

During our return flight over the North Sea I contemplate the sense or otherwise of such attacks. While I can rely on Hans to make

* UFA (Universum Film AG) was one of the foremost German film companies before and during the war years. (Tr.)

every effort to find an important military target for our bombs, I also know that it is quite possible that our terrible ammunition has been unloaded somewhere where it would have no effect at all. Then again, what if it has hit a residential district or even a hospital? This war really is a gruesome business. But I am sure the others have the same problem: there might well be a British airman pondering along the same lines as I am right now.

I land Cäsar softly alongside the flare path in Gilze at exactly 0310 hrs. My crew give me the usual compliments: they are obviously just as pleased to be safely back on the ground as I am.

We were in the air five hours and 20 minutes, and it is almost impossible to straighten our limbs again.

28 April 1941
My 50th operational flight!

We take off at 2210 hrs with two 1,000 kg aerial mines destined for Portsmouth. Although our experiences over there have not been very good we are pleased about this trip because the largest part of the outward and return flights takes place over our own territory.

According to the prevailing wind I take off in an easterly direction, then go into a wide reverse turn slowly gaining altitude before flying on the opposite course direction south-west. On the way out we fly once more past the whole red-white-green light display of Gilze-Rijen before leaving it for the darkness in the west. Cäsar is well trimmed, I have set the engines to cruising revs and switched on the autopilot. In short: everything is in the best possible order aboard.

Hans has put away his maps and slide rule and sits in his usual posture, upright, with his eyes shut, next to me. I feel very tired and light a cigarette, contemplating the familiar constellations in the sky while having a smoke. The night is so quiet and peaceful that, assisted by the automatic pilot Cäsar can fly on its own and steadily gain altitude without my touching the control column. I want to ask Hans how long we have to fly before reaching Cherbourg but then decide not to do so, knowing full well he will let me know just the same in good time. Apart from that it would create some disturbance for me if suddenly there was all that fumbling around with lights, direction finder, calculations and cursing, so I leave it be

– and fall asleep! Right over the area where only a short while ago we were so effectively shot up by our own AA guns!

The sudden howling-up of the port engine in the moment when the supercharger is coupled in by the automatic control shocks me awake. A glance at the instruments: we are 4,200 metres high! The engine temperatures are much too low because the radiator flaps are still open, the fuel service tanks are nearly empty because nobody has activated the fuel pump-over system – a real mess! Hans is hanging in his harness next to me, leaning with his head against the cabin glazing – fast asleep. They are all asleep! I have to literally wake up each one of them individually, Hans, Hein and Theo. God Almighty, we must have slept for hours like this! It is high time we did something: had we continued flying asleep as we were we would have passed quietly and cleanly into the other world at higher altitude without our oxygen masks. Where are we? What time is it?

But first we put on our masks and, to be fully awake and clear my head, I gulp down pure oxygen for a while before regulating it to normal mixture. Then I fish out two Dextro-Energen tablets from my knee pocket: they always wake me up in no time!

And Hans, the inhuman monster! Although he knows full well the dozy predicament we are in, all he can do is curse to himself while fumbling about for the direction finder with his shaded pocket torch, taking ages before drawing those few lines on the map held on his knees. That done, he curses some more: 'God-damned idiots!', before stating calmly: 'Hold this course for another five minutes, then change to 355 degrees!' as if nothing has happened.

We arrive at the target twenty minutes late and are greeted by the usual fireworks. There is no hanging about this time: bombs away, right in the middle of it, and then homewards. We land back in Gilze at 0150 hrs after almost four hours' flying.

During our long flight back the conversation aboard was naturally about our dozing off, and it led to a quarrel. It was really my fault because I rebuked the other three although I had slumbered for at least for an hour myself. Be as it may, one thing led to another, and I told them they were probably dozing every time we made our long outward flight over the sea, and that is why it was always so quiet aboard. Then they all picked on me in return. For a start, I had been asleep the same as they were and, secondly, it was

A Ju 88A-4 of 7./KG 30 (part of III Gruppe) during deployment on a southerly airfield.

Ju 88A bombers on a temporary landing field.

high time to tell me that things could not go on the way they had been any longer: night after night on arduous operations followed by either 'pleasure flights' or some special trips by day.

'Every time when Stoffregen says, "Well, Stahl, is it all right for tonight?" you say yes, but nobody cares what the crew thinks!'

It is hard for me to argue on that point. It is true that all other crews are flying far less than us. 'But I would like to remind you of one thing, that we are always afraid and unsure of ourselves after a longer break in flying – for instance, after a leave! Why do you think it is that other crews are falling down one after the other, over there, and here too? It is either because they don't know how to do it, or because they have gone soft, that's why!'

But my crew just goes on grumbling: 'We are not such packhorses as you are. And we have simply come to the end, and don't want any more part in it.'

I try once more: 'Look, I am pretty well all in myself, and because of that alone it would be wrong to give up if we want to stay alive!'

But when the recriminations became more subjective and even malicious I simply refuse to answer and end the argument for my part by telling them to look for another captain.

However, the things are smooth over again already in the bus on our way back to the monastery: we will go on flying together as a crew after all!

29 April 1941
Just 24 hours after our last operational flight we are once again on our way to the Island.

Barely awake, I drive out to the airfield to try my luck in organising something to fly. After what took place the night before, I do not take any of my own crew with me.

The TO (Technical Officer of the Gruppe) was really pleased he had a pilot on hand who would carry out the three workshop test flights that needed to be done. I must admit all this was a bit out of spite towards my crew, but it satisfied me, anyhow!

And then it was back to operational readiness, and now we are flying in our old oil slick of the night before, direction Cherbourg radio beacon. From there, it is across the Channel, only this time to Plymouth instead of Portsmouth.

The aerial mines in the target area are exploding at such short intervals it is impossible to determine the position of our own deliveries. The fires down below must be devastating. Then again, here at Plymouth the British have managed to lay on various dummy fires that are so big and deceptive one is really hard put to distinguish between them.

On the way out we are caught by a sudden and well-laid barrage of AA fire, but save ourselves by a steep turn.

During our return flight the whole crew behaves like a happy family. Everybody makes an effort to be most friendly and cooperative, and it's a sheer pleasure to be their captain.

2 May 1941

A concentration of ships has been reported outside the Humber estuary, apparently scared of our mines or forced to wait for some other reason until the entrance is free.

I take off together with the commander of our Gruppe to carry out an attack during the final hours of twilight.

We chase across the sea in very bad weather in close formation, but then lose each other shortly before reaching the target area, and I have to continue on my own. The ships are not where they were reported to be and I have to search around for several costly minutes until I spot them. It is already almost dark when they give themselves away by some wild shooting. By then it is impossible to carry out a proper 'aimed' attack and I have to fly through the fireworks at low level trusting my luck. Under such conditions, of course, things go awry. Although I manage to release my bombs onto one of those fire-spitting pots it is already so dark that we cannot even attempt to observe the effects.

Later on our commander tells us he had no better luck than us. He had seen us being fired at and then flown an attack in the same way as we did – 'aiming over the thumb', so to speak – which is pretty hopeless when attacking shipping targets.

7 May 1941

Fly, sleep, eat and wait – that is how the last few days have gone by. The targets included Liverpool and Glasgow again, and Hull – our bombers were out night after night. And every time the operation was a success.

On the other hand, the opposition by enemy night fighters is becoming increasingly more unpleasant and the AA guns fire control system has been so improved that when someone has been caught he is very hard put to get away again.

To date I have completed sixty operational flights against the Island, almost all of them by night. At times I shudder to think that on average our new crews survive only three to four night operations.

Tonight it is again Hull, but this is my night off. We intend to go into the town this evening and partake of a few glasses of something good. Just as we are about to leave our billets Völling calls me to the telephone. It is Stoffregen: 'I am sorry about this, but you will have to fly again tonight. The Air Corps has been snooping around and found out that formations are making arbitrary decisions on which crews are held back from operations and there has been a hell of a scandal about this!'

'And if I am just simply ill, Sir?'

'But you are not!'

'Not me, but my crew. The fellows are at an end, they are all in. Recently we were all fast asleep for half an operational flight!'

'I know all that, but it cannot be helped, you just have to fly!'

During our briefing Stoffregen brings up the subject again in front of the whole Staffel. He explains that Hermann Göring himself has ordered that night operations against the Island must not only be continued at present intensity but increased in strength by all possible means. High Command has acquired information that it is only a matter of weeks before the Island people will be ready to give in.

On hearing this, Hans comments loud enough for all those standing nearby to hear, that maybe 'Fatty' and his red-trousered staff scribes believe all this, but 'They should fly over there themselves, then they would see who is about to collapse!' I nudge Hans in the ribs.

'But it's true!' he shouts at me.

There is dead silence in the briefing room, until Stoffregen speaks up again as if nothing had happened: 'Well then, have a good trip!'

Despite our initially depressed mood the night flight to Hull turns out to be one of the most interesting and successful we have experienced so far.

It is a clear moonlit night, and visibility is good. We manage to play tricks on the night fighters and the AA guns are as tame as in the old days. By that I mean they let themselves be conducted from above and are happily shooting wherever I want them to think we are. The bright moon makes the night almost into a day, and the town lies spread out underneath us like a picture postcard.

Hans draws my attention to a large block of buildings not far from the port – the oil mills. Right – we will take them in a dive! Before my crew can voice their protests I have put Cäsar on its head and down we go from about 5,000 metres. All this being so sudden I have to make preparations for the dive while already committed to it: shut the radiator flaps, switch on booster pumps, extend dive brakes, and trim the aircraft.

'Hans – keep on letting me know the altitude!': I dare not go too low because of the barrage balloons.

At 2,000 metres altitude the building complex lies clear and steady in my reflex sight, but I still bide my time. Hans now gives me the altitude every 50 metres instead of every 100 metres as before. Quite naturally he has become nervous: a dive-bombing attack at night is not exactly a picnic.

Then, at 1,550 metres altitude, I lift our nose and let go of my two BM 1,000s. The automatic pull-out device couples in, and we are pressed down into our seats. Then comes the familiar grey curtain – stars in the night sky – AA fire – and then nothing but away from the place!

Flying a zig-zagging course southwards I manage to evade the light AA shells that are reaching out for us. The two flashes of exploding bombs that are followed immediately by a flaring up of a fire in the oil mills we ascribe to our attack, although we did not manage a clear look at the results.

Cäsar is now so light and climbs so beautifully that I decide to fly near the target once more to try for a better observation of the results of our attack. Other aircraft which have arrived in the meantime are diverting the AA fire, and so we fly over the town for the second time. There can be no doubt about it now: the oil mills

A *Kette* of Ju 88A bombers in close formation.

Fully bombed-up Ju 88A-4s of KG 30 share an operational airfield with a He 111H-6 of another unit.

are blazing in two places, and soon this will grow into one big conflagration. The following crews will have no difficulties in aiming their bombs.

We land back in Gilze at 0245 hrs after four hours of flying. 'Well, Heinis, wasn't that something?' I comment while carefully touching my brake pedals before taxying to a standstill.

Cheerful and not a little proud of ourselves we drive home as quickly as possible, without waiting for the last machines to land – not to mention waiting until we know who has to be counted missing this time.

We are the first crew back at Mariahof where our good Dutch kitchen ladies receive us with the obligatory milk soup. I shall never forget how touchingly concerned for us these Dutch ladies always were. They would cry for joy when we came back safe and sound, and would grieve when a crew was missing as if they were their own sons. It did not matter if they had to be in the kitchen 24 hours at a stretch: they would be there, ready to read our every wish in our eyes.

I am woken up by Völling about midday. I must have slept like a log! 'You have to report to the Command post with your small overnight baggage as quickly as possible. You have to fly to Germany with the Bf 108!'

Well, I am quite sure there is enough time for me to have a shave and a wash before reporting. Outside, I find out that I have to fly some 'Home front' Colonel back to Halberstadt. The machine is already standing there, and my good Colonel looks at me in a reproving manner because it seems he had to wait for me. Not that it worries me – I am certainly not going to hurry for him.

First, I telephone Stoffregen and obtain permission to stay overnight. After that I carry out my pre-flight preparations in emphasised detail and then pick up my small leather suitcase and walk out to the Bf 108. My 'sandbag' follows in my footsteps, dragging his large holdall full of 'booty' with a displeased look on his face. He has to make another trip to collect all his hoard.

I have strapped myself in in the meantime. I am in a nasty mood and just waiting for a word or a gesture on my passenger's part to tell him what I think of his ilk. The character now sitting in our machine is exactly the type of staff jackass we operational crews hate like a pest. His chest is daintily decorated with the ribbon of the War Service Cross, 2nd Class, and the Air Gunner's badge. Some air gunner indeed!

While taxying out to my take-off point I happen to glance at my suitcase and suddenly realise to my horror that it is not mine at all but belongs to an Oberleutnant, as I can tell from the attached tag. Both suitcases are so much alike that they look the same at a glance. Fortunately I got to know at Flight control that this officer is flying with a Bf 110 to Düsseldorf, and he must have picked up my suitcase by mistake. Just at that moment I can see him taking off, and there is no way I can recall him now. My only chance is to follow him as quickly as I can, hoping to catch up with him at Düsseldorf.

I give full throttle on the spot and take off obliquely across the airfield. The Bf 110 is at least twice as fast as its small sister, my 108, and every minute is now precious!

I land in Düsseldorf straight towards the Flight control office, jump out and run. And there comes the Oberleutnant from Gilze, strolling towards me with my suitcase in his hand. It is obvious he has not noticed anything yet. We have a good laugh about it and wish each other a pleasant sojourn in the homeland.

At the Flight control office nobody minds my 'illegal' landing and I can immediately continue on my way to Halberstadt with my sullen 'hamster'.

There I have two hours to spare before my train is due to depart and decide to get something to eat at the local mess. Quite inadvertently, I happen to land there among a party of older officers who are celebrating something and are already in high spirits. I am more or less compelled to take a seat and join in, and of course am questioned, which results in my person – and the whole of our 'Englandgeschwader' being celebrated in great style. They even provide a car to take me to the railway station.

CHAPTER TWELVE

A Change of Base

11 May 1941

The night war against England is over – at least for us. We are to be transferred to Aalborg in Jutland, Denmark, within the next few days.

In the meantime, our machines are being thoroughly overhauled. Cäsar receives completely new engines and, in addition, has all special installations for flare bombs taken out and the second fuselage fuel tank fitted back in. Externally, all sooty camouflage is removed.

The 4. and 5. Staffeln are leaving already today while we of 6.Staffel will not be ready for a few days yet.

We leave behind us nine hard months here at Gilze-Rijen, and the dammed-up tension is now unloading. We are celebrating something or other all the time, and one can almost feel the relief in the air.

In the evening Leutnant Harmel gives a special performance in the mess, a 'one-man show' as it were, a re-enacting for us the recent memorable visit by our Commanding General together with Feldmarschall Milch. Harmel plays the roles to perfection: the lining-up of our Staffeln and the technical personnel in parade order on the tarmac; the waiting lasting for hours; the excited sergeant-major of the airfield service company; reports to the Staffelkapitäne; reports to the Gruppe commander – it is all there.

Then the landing of the General's Ju 52/3m transport. Report of our commander to the Feldmarschall, followed by an inspection walk along the lined-up men. The occasional fatherly and benevolent question to some soldier, the stammered reply – we are doubled up from laughter. This lighthearted 'action replay' is so well done and I laugh so much I have pains in my midriff and tears are streaming down my face. No more, please – that's enough! But Harmel is now at full steam and has reached the high spot of his performance: the address by the General.

'You are the pride of the nation ... Fatherland looks to you ... With unheard-of sacrifices ... In a few weeks the enemy will ... For that very reason ... And do not ease up right now, at this moment ... I have seen reports from which it appears this or that Gruppe is showing signs of growing soft ... That is cowardice in the face of the enemy! I will take the necessary measures ...!' –

Time and again Harmel throws in various asides from the lined-up men, spoken as muttered comments or just 'thinking aloud': – 'Arsehole!' – 'You're a coward yourself!' – 'Hail, Hail!' – 'Too true!' –

We realise only later how macabre the whole performance basically was. But it was great fun at the time.

During the half hour it takes us to walk back to our billets at night I think again about Harmel's play-acting. Only a few weeks have gone by since that visit by the General, and I recall very clearly how we were all stimulated – incited would be a better word for it – to hold out and increase our efforts for only a short while longer. The enemy was just about all in. That was a few weeks ago. Today, we are giving up ourselves and thus admitting our defeat after all.

Has the Feldmarschall really lied to us?

22 May 1941
We are transferring to Aalborg today. The take-off is set for 1600 hrs, so that we have plenty of time to bid farewell.

No one goes willingly into an uncertain future. During the past nine months here we had felt so well, and settled in so much – at least as far as conditions essential for life are concerned – that we find it very hard to take leave of the place.

The local population had always been correct and, mostly, friendly disposed towards us. Our kitchen ladies are crying their eyes out. When the bus drives up to collect us the bell on the cloister roof rings out in farewell.

A short while later we roar low across the familiar buildings and see the Dutch kitchen ladies still waving to us – and then we are gone.

For several days before our departure I had sat almost without pause in our Ju 52/3m transport. I had been detailed to fly to Germany, Denmark and southern France, and enjoyed every minute of it. It was like flying in peacetime again, sitting behind the controls of that big good-natured kite without worrying about the enemy AA defences or unknown weather.

On my flights over Denmark I could not help noticing that practically every house had hoisted their national flag. It was clear they did not like us at all, and were using every opportunity to show it to us.

23 May 1941
We stay in Aalborg just one night before transferring to Stavanger in Norway today.

It is being said we will be operating from there mainly against shipping along the British East Coast. The transfer flight offers us everything that makes up bad weather: there is a westerly storm with showers, and the cloud base is generally less than 50 metres off ground level. Only three machines from the whole Staffel manage to get through: Stoffregen, Scheller, and myself. Due to the storm and bad visibility Scheller makes a crash landing on arrival at Stavanger. The other crews turn back. Balance sheet for the day: three crashes (two machines crashed after returning to Aalborg), one badly injured crew, and one broken-up Staffel! Neither Stoffregen nor the crews are to blame for this. We tried to convince the commanding headquarters of the senselessness of a transfer flight in this weather to the last moment, but in vain. The orders came from the Luftwaffe Operations Staff and had to be carried out at all costs. It is so simple to be a General Staff officer!

Things have changed quite a bit at Stavanger since I was here last for a brief visit a year ago. The airfield has been extended, although the accommodation has not yet caught up with the completed runways. We are living in simple new wooden barracks, without electricity or running water. The walls are painted with some paint that stinks of fish oil, and everything is somewhat dreary and uncomfortable. Cigarettes are in short supply and of bad quality, and there is hardly anything to drink.

At Stavanger, we relieve KG 26 which supposedly can no longer keep up with the demands with their lame He 111s. Apart from that the Gruppe* has reportedly lost 13 crews within a few weeks and is now completely 'flown out'.

1 June 1941
From 24 May until today we have been in almost constant readiness for operations against shipping around England despite the fact that our Staffel consists only of fragments. But it was all just so much strain: the weather remained constantly bad. We have to admire the weather reconnaissance crews who are out over the sea for many hours every day and are doing an excellent job of work.

Today, at Whitsuntide, I take off alone on my first operation against shipping near the northerly coast of Scotland. These ships have probably been reported by the Navy and I am to try at all costs to get at them, but it proves impossible. I have to pull up into the clouds shortly before reaching the outer Scottish islands to avoid smashing into their high rocky cliffs. In the clouds I keep on climbing in a westerly direction until I come out on top, and then we try to find the area where Scapa Flow should be. Apparently we are just about right because we suddenly draw some hefty fire from heavy AA guns. Here I press haphazardly on the button and let my bombs drop into the clouds.

After a four-hour-long strenuous flight I then manage to sneak through the low-flying cloud tatters just above the boiling sea near the Norwegian coast and am hard put not to miss the rain-lashed runway at Stavanger.

3 June 1941
Once again we are flying at low level over the 'big pond'. Echeloned behind me are Feldwebeln Guggenmos and Hachenberg. We took off at about 2310 hrs to attack a convoy that should be in map-square 5933-15 West. At this time it is still bright daylight up here in the North and even two and half hours later, when we are getting near the Shetlands, it is still dangerously light. Anything but fighters now!

Our navigation has been accurate 'to the metre': in low-level

---

* In late May 1941 *Stab* I and III/KG 26 were at Stravanger. (Tr.)

flight we almost hit the small island that lies exactly half way between the Orkneys in the south and Shetlands in the north. We can see the mountains of the island groups as we continue flying westwards at low level before turning south. There we have Cape Wrath as our base point; from there on we fly eastwards, with the steep rocky walls of the Scottish coast looking down on us from the right all the way. We are following the reported course of the convoy and right at the estimated spot smoke clouds appear on the horizon.

Surprisingly quickly they turn into ships, about 30 or more, and I press down even lower to avoid being spotted too soon. With iron discipline, Guggenmos and Hachenberg are keeping close formation with me. Then, in the last moment, I ram the throttles fully forward and pull up. Apparently nobody has spotted us yet, but there is no time for lengthy contemplation. The whole situation, bright twilight and low-lying clouds demands quick action, and each of us picks the closest boat. From a flat turn to port I attack, selecting without much reflection the last ship steaming in the second row. From 500 metres altitude I put my Ju 88 into a flat glide and watch the ship quickly growing bigger in my dimly luminous reflector-sight. I set the aiming point square amidships, and let go.

The fireworks break out beneath us simultaneously with the release of my bombs. They have spotted us too late, but are now giving us everything they have got from all sides.

Rid of our load, we get out of the immediate danger zone quite quickly. Looking back, I can see that Sepp and Willi too have managed to approach their targets undisturbed and are again there, to port and starboard behind me. Closing in, we signal to each other with raised thumbs that everything is in order.

Theo reports from his ventral gondola that the last of our four bombs must have hit the ship's side. The other three fell a bit short, as evidenced by three towering columns of water. The last bomb on the other hand has given rise to a black cloud of an explosion – a hit. 'How big?' I ask the crew. After a lengthy debate we average our estimates to approximately 5,000 gross registered tons.

On the way past the Orkneys report their presence with a shower of heavy AA shells – a reminder of our nocturnal flights over the island.

I receive confirmation of my hit after landing back at the base:

The author in 1942 when he was awarded the German Cross in Gold.

Willi Hachenberg's crew were able to follow my attack and report most accurately. Unfortunately both he and Sepp just missed their own targets.

5 June 1941

With the Bf 108 to Oslo-Fornebu. I am supposed to collect secret courier material which will detail our future operational area. A mechanic accompanies me for the trip.

The flight over the mountains turns into an experience in its own right. While in Germany at this time of the year the temperature is almost summery, here in Norway the mountains are still covered in snow down to 1,000 metres altitude, and the numerous mountain lakes are still frozen. From the air one gets the impression of a lonely, almost uninhabited land. Only rarely are there some houses scattered in the deeply snowed-up valleys. I have to ask myself, how do these people survive? How do they live? Where do their children go to school? Do they know at all what is going on in the world outside?

In Oslo I am taken by car to Holmenkollen where the Luftflotte* has its headquarters. There are sentries, orderlies and General Staff officers all over the place. So this is where the war is made!

I am taken to 'my' department where four heavy parcels are already waiting for me. Before I can collect them I have to undergo another verification of my documents and identity. A major in red breeches is rather mocking because no officer has been detailed for this courier flight. At home in Stavanger we have only a few very young Leutnanten and a Staffelkapitän who is overloaded and, apart from that, badly in need of a rest. But do they care here?

'If you don't deliver the things at home according to regulations it will cost you your head!'

Stupid 'pretty boy', I think to myself. I also manage a quick look at the paper held by the Orderly Officer which presumably lists the contents of my packets: Soviet Union, nothing but Soviet Union!

I land my little kite back at Stavanger at about 2000 hrs. The return flight was thoroughly 'spiced' by my new knowledge. Why should the war spread to the Soviet Union as well? We have a

---

* Luftflotte 5, commanded by General Hans-Jürgen Stumpff. (Tr.)

Sunset over the Atlantic.

non-aggression pact! And the Soviets supply us with oil and grain and are thus supporting us against England. How could one still understand this world?

That night I can find no sleep at all. I would gladly have talked to Stoffregen, who must be as confused as I am.

In the night four of our machines are once more on the way to the Scottish coast. Sepp Guggenmos manages to hit and damage a 5,000-ton ship, and I am pleased for him.

6 June 1941
Together with Stoffregen I 'enlivened' an exercise of locally-stationed infantry by some simulated low-level attacks. It was great fun!

For the 'night' (there really is none up here in the north) we are again ordered to be in operational readiness.

Around 1900 hrs Stoffregen calls me to the command post. I am to lead a formation of five aircraft to attack a gathering of ships discovered in a fjord on the western coast of Scotland. The place is called Loch Ewe. From the latest aerial reconnaissance photographs spread out on the table it is evident that a large number of ships have hidden away in the deeply cut fjord surrounded by high rocky cliffs. It would seem these ships will be unloaded there because use of the ports at the East Coast and the approaches to them have been too costly in the number of ships lost – surely a success for our aerial mining operations. Places like Hull and the Thames spring to mind.

We discuss every detail of how best to carry out the outward flight, the attack itself and the return flight. Stoffregen leaves all detailed preparations to me, and I am similarly excited and proud when I call together the crew allotted to me. They are captained by Feldwebel Schenk, Leutnant Harmel, Unteroffizier Scheller and Unteroffizier Hachenberg. I know them well and all, with the exception of Scheller, have had some operational experience.

This is the first time I have conducted a briefing as the leader responsible for a formation, and a day to remember.

The operation takes place exactly as prepared and discussed. We take off at 2220 hrs, fly at low level over the sea, reach the critical 'sneak-through' point between the Orkneys and the Shetlands, and then continue westwards for a while before turning south towards Cape Wrath on the northern coast of Scotland. From there on we climb slowly over the land in the direction of our target. It is long past midnight when we complete the final part of our target approach flight. Despite the time it is still so light that we can recognise Loch Ewe 30 km distant from our altitude of less than 2,000 m.

I wonder, and then become rather uneasy about why we have not seen any signs of defences yet. This is certainly contrary to my previous experiences over the southern half of the British Isles.

My four followers behave impeccably, climb steadily and remain in loose formation behind me. I keep over the land to attack in westerly direction against the somewhat lighter side of the sky. Tension mounts aboard as we get nearer the target and begin to distinguish details in the inlet. There are ships and more ships of all sizes! We have reached 3,000 metres altitude when the distance is just right to start our run.

According to our previous agreement we are now to go into a 'prowling' flight, each pilot selecting his own target before attacking. We all do just that – except Scheller, who scurries on ahead into the bay at full throttle and thus completely 'tramples our salad underfoot'.*

As a result the moment of surprise is lost and we are received with a veritable hail of AA fire. I am certainly not going into that! By then I have already reached my intended wing-over point for the attack, but turn around instead. There is now absolutely no chance of carrying out a successful attack by diving into that red wall of tracers. My intention is to attempt another attack from a turn to starboard, and Lady Luck smiles on me!

While the others are diving and drawing the concentrated AA fire on themselves, Hans and I simultaneously detect a particularly large ship in the middle of the bay, standing some distance apart from the rest of the herd. Another thing we notice is that it remains completely quiet and does not participate in the general shooting.

---

* Colloquial expression used by Luftwaffe aircrews generally meaning messed-up opportunity or chance. (Tr.)

That ship belongs to us! I level off and dive on it without bothering about my dive brakes. Hans reads off the altitude while I have some trouble with the reflector sight which I had set too bright, but I manage to turn the dimming knob while diving. Then the 'fat pot' is clearly in my sight, enormously big, and I press the bomb release button. I have to pull out of the dive manually, because the automatic pull-out device will only work when the dive brakes are out, and this takes some doing. I pull back on the control column with all my might while the dark cliffs grow higher into the sky left and right of me. For God's sake, don't let us smash into the water now!

By straining every muscle in my body I finally manage to level off just a few metres over the waves and shoot through the narrow rocky gateway of the bay out to the open sea.

Theo shouts something unintelligible on the intercom while Cäsar climbs steeply into the pale sky. What has happened?

'Man, Peter – we have hit it! It is an enormous ship!'

Great news – but at first I am fully occupied getting my aircraft and myself in order before I can even reflect on our success. Then I hear the details from Theo and Leutnant Merbeller who has replaced Hein, who is away ill tonight.

We return to the scene of our attack once more, flying past at a respectable distance. Now I can see for myself that 'our' ship is obviously badly hit. It seems to be listing, and smaller vessels are scurrying around it in the water. That's enough – now home!

Both Theo and Merbeller had observed that all four bombs hit immediately at the ship's side, and no vessel could survive that.

We are the last to land at Stavanger and report 'One big ship badly damaged!' We simplified our return flight over the Scottish Highlands by whizzing low along the famous Loch Ness, a nice straight run.

It was the first operational flight for Leutnant Merbeller, who is normally our Signals Officer at the base. Trouble is, in his excitement he spoiled all our pleasure by jabbering on the radio all the way back over the North Sea. It would seem that everything he saw and felt he just had to share with us. That is understandable, but can become annoying and sometimes even dangerous, because on these flights we are over enemy territory practically the whole time.

On such occasions, any distraction from concentrating on the task in hand by each crew member means a reduction in safety for all. Unfortunately it is impossible to completely avoid having a 'foreign body' aboard now and then.

7 June 1941

We did not get to bed until 0700 hrs this morning, but I am awakened by Völling already at 1000 hrs with a request to report to Oberleutnant Schneider at the Command Post. He is preparing a specially detailed report based on our individual statements of last night and wanted to ask me a number of additional questions. Apparently our observations had caused quite a stir. A reconnaissance aircraft was already on the way there and is expected back soon, hopefully with some good photographs.

By late afternoon Oberleutnant Schneider has the photos taken over Loch Ewe on his table. These not only confirm our statements of last night but also show clearly 'my' ship under water. Experts have estimated it to be of about 15,000 gross registered tons. This results in the usual 'film run' on such occasions: congratulations and teleprinter messages from all kinds of 'big names' along the lines of 'Well done, carry on in the same way!' with suitable measures of liquid encouragement.

I get more pleasure out of the honest enthusiasm of our technical personnel led by Oberwerkmeister Oberfeldwebel Preuss.

As an official confirmation of my success I receive a magnificent attestation from the Geschwader, the third such document I have earned so far.

8 June 1941

Another black day today: Oberleutnant Wolff and Leutnant Hick are missing. Both had the same operational task as I the night before. I have to fly out at 0240 hrs to search for them. We have no news of Oberleutnant Wolff, but Leutnant Hick managed to radio an SOS message giving his position near the Shetlands.

I fly past the islands in daylight hardly 20 kilometres away. I know there is an airfield nearby with fighters which have probably shot down Hick. Nevertheless, we search the sea according to schedule until there is only enough fuel left in our tanks for the return flight.

But we search in vain. Apart from a few fishing boats, some of which fire at us and have no doubt reported us to their centre long ago, there is nothing: no yellow dinghy, no signal flares, no coloured patches on the water.*

I realise only on the return flight, when we have left the zone of immediate danger behind us, that I am perspiring all over. The dangerous search in a narrow area over the sea under constant enemy observation has done me in.

We never heard anything of Arno Wolff. He and his crew, Feldwebel Erler, Unteroffizier Weber and another Feldwebel, a newcomer not yet known to me, were among the old hands on the Staffel. We are hoping that at least they managed to stay alive. It is known to us that the British air-sea rescue service is efficient and does everything possible to rescue ditched aircrews from the 'big pond'. Of course, this is not done simply for humanitarian reasons but mainly to prevent our own air-sea rescue service finding the crews and bringing them back again.

It happens quite often that both opposing air-sea rescue services run a regular competition to be first on the spot.

---

* All Luftwaffe airmen detailed to fly over waters carried special packets of very fine coloured powder that spread quickly over the water surface when the packet was torn. (Tr.)

This concludes the first part of the author's diary. The second part relates the story of the author's operations over the Soviet Union; the problems caused by the bitterly cold winter of 1941/42; his participation in raids on Archangel and the Murmansk railway; his baling-out from a defective aircraft 60 miles behind the enemy lines, the seemingly endless lonely walk back towards his own lines, hide-and-seek and then rescue when near total exhaustion, and the unexpected reunion of the whole crew; his special operations to assist Finnish long-range patrols far behind the enemy lines; attacks on convoys; his sudden transfer to the Mediterranean and North Africa late in 1942, when the author is finally promoted to Leutnant and becomes Technical Officer of his Gruppe; supply and other problems in 1943-44; new tactics with the Ju 88; the retreat in Italy; end of the Luftwaffe bomber arm and orders to retrain as fighter pilots. But there is another choice, and the author takes it. He joins the famous KG 200 – Hitler's renowned 'Spy Geschwader', or the Luftwaffe sabotage wing.

Glossary

Luftwaffe units
As there are no exact equivalents, this translation has kept the original German unit designations such as Staffel, Gruppe and Geschwader. Depending on its role and operational conditions, a Staffel could have anything from 9 to 16 aircraft, although a bomber Staffel would normally average 10-12; a Gruppe, which was the basic operational unit of the Luftwaffe, comprised three to four Staffeln, and a Geschwader had a nominal strength of three to four Gruppen, with the temporary IV Gruppe used as an operational training unit. The actual operational strength of a Kampfgeschwader or KG (loosely: Bomber Wing) was usually lower than its establishment due to combat losses and outstanding personnel and materiél replacements.

The Staffeln within a Geschwader were indicated by Arabic numerals, the Gruppen – by Roman numerals. Thus 6./KG 30 = 6.Staffel of KG 30 (part of II/KG 30), and II/KG 30 = II Gruppe of KG 30.

Ranks
The following table lists the equivalent Luftwaffe and British/ American air force ranks. A German pilot could be an ordinary Flieger (Airman) or Gefreiter (LAC) whereas an RAF pilot had to be at least a Sergeant and a USAAF pilot, a Second Lieutenant. It should also be borne in mind that in the Luftwaffe the command powers and responsibility were according to appointment and not

the rank, eg a Leutnant could be Staffelkapitän (Staffel leader) and, on operations, have command powers over pilots of higher rank.

Luftwaffe	*RAF*	*USAAF*
Generalfeldmarschall	Marshal of the RAF	General (five star)
Generaloberst	Air Chief Marshal	General (four star)
General der Flieger	Air Marshal	Lieutenant General
Generalleutnant	Air Vice Marshal	Major General
Oberst	Group Captain	Colonel
Oberstleutnant	Wing Commander	Lieutenant Colonel
Major	Squadron Leader	Major
Hauptmann	Flight Lieutenant	Captain
Oberleutnant	Flying Officer	1st Lieutenant
Leutnant	Pilot Officer	2nd Lieutenant
Oberfeldwebel	Flight Sergeant	Master Sergeant
Feldwebel	Sergeant	Sergeant
Unteroffizier	Corporal	Corporal
Gefreiter	Leading Aircraftman	Private 1st Class
Flieger	Airman	Private

The Junkers Ju 88

by Alex Vanags-Baginskis

The Ju 88 was an outstanding combat aircraft by any standards and, thanks to its good performance and adaptability, became the true backbone of the Luftwaffe in the Second World War. It was also the most produced German multi-purpose aircraft type. Of the slightly more than 15,000 Ju 88s of all versions built between 1939 and 1945 some 9,120 were completed as bombers, 1,910 as long-range reconnaissance aircraft, and about 3,950 as night fighters, including several hundred heavy day fighters (*Zerstörer*), most of which were later equipped with radar and used operationally as night fighters.

In addition, at least 250 older or repaired (and later brand-new airframes on the production line) were converted during the last year of fighting into unmanned explosive carriers guided to their target by a pilot in a detachable pick-a-back fighter.

The Ju 88 was a very advanced military aeroplane at the time of its appearance and, as related in this book, was designed as a 'one-man' aircraft to be operated as a bomber by the pilot alone if necessary. Apart from that its construction incorporated a number of novel features that made the Ju 88 initially a demanding aircraft to control and maintain. Once mastered however, the Ju 88 was a rewarding aircraft to fly and what is more, generally successful in the various roles it was adapted for and used in operationally.

As a daytime horizontal- and dive-bomber the Ju 88 fared far better during the Battle of Britain than its contemporaries He 111 and Do 17Z, although its defensive armament too was found wanting. This was gradually rectified on later models. When flown by a competent pilot, the Ju 88 could also be often relied on in for its speed and manoeuvrability to avoid interception by day as well as during the following Blitz of 1940/41 – a situation that changed in 1942 when the RAF night fighters began using air interception radar on a larger scale.

During the period covered by this translation of the first part of his diary the author flew operationally the Ju 88A-1, A-5 and A-4, of which the Ju 88A-4 (which followed the A-5 in production) was the most widely built and used bomber version.

The Ju 88 originated in 1935 as a result of an official specification requesting a three-seat high-speed bomber. The Junkers concern had every intention of winning this contract and engaged W.H. Evert and A. Gassner, two engineers who had acquired considerable experience in light metal stressed-skin construction in the USA, to design the new bomber. The Ju 88 was the second of two parallel studies (the alternative Ju 85 had a twin fin/rudder configuration) and incorporated the latest aviation technology.

The first prototype, the Ju 88V1* was flown on 21 December 1936 powered by two Daimler-Benz 600Aa inline engines with annual radiators, and the test results with this and the following two prototypes were so promising that preparations were put in hand for a large scale production to commence in spring 1938. The Ju 88V4, powered by two Junkers Jumo 211A engines that became standard, was first flown on 2 February 1938 and introduced the characteristic 'bee's eye' nose section glazing of optically flat panels, and the ventral defensive gun gondola.

In the meantime the dive bombing method of attack had gained strong official support and the Technical Branch of the RLM (Reichsluftfahrtministerium, the German State Air Ministry) requested this capability from the Ju 88 as well. Accordingly, initial production plans were shelved until the first two modified and restressed dive bomber prototypes (Ju 88V8 and V9) could be tested beginning October 1938.

Meanwhile, in line with the official policy to get the most publicity for the resurrected German air force the fifth Ju 88 prototype was streamlined and, described as 'Ju 85S', established a new 1,000 km (621 mile) closed circuit speed record in March 1939 carrying a 2,000 kg (4,410 lb) payload at an average speed of 517 km/h (321.25 mph).

* V – *Versuchs*, experimental. (Tr.)

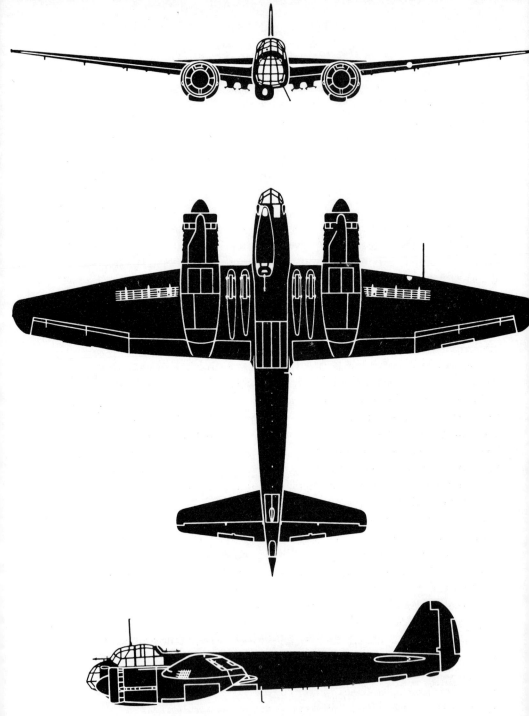

Silhouette of the Ju 88

The first pre-production Ju 88A-0 bombers were delivered to a service trials unit early in 1939. At the same time the Junkers concern introduced the 'Takt' system of production ordered by General Udet the previous autumn, whereby the construction was broken down into components manufactured by several other plants and assembled elsewhere.

The first Ju 88A-1 series production bombers were delivered in autumn 1939, and the service trials unit was redesignated I/KG 25 as the first Luftwaffe formation equipped with the new Ju 88 bomber. In September 1939 its designation was changed to I/KG 30, and the famous Adler-Geschwader was born. Because of its speed, manoeuvrability and load-carrying capacity great things were expected of the new Ju 88, but its advanced features took some time to assimilate in service.

Its first operational sortie was a raid on British warships in the Firth of Forth on 26 September 1939 when hits were mistakenly claimed on the aircraft carrier HMS *Ark Royal*. The first two Ju 88A-1s to fall to British fighters were shot down during the second raid by I/KG 30 on the Firth of Forth on 16 October 1939.

Although production of the new bomber gradually gained momentum the early Ju 88A-1s were so highly stressed that strict limits had to be imposed on high speed manoeuvres. An attendant if temporary problem was undercarriage failure on landing.

With the availability of more aircraft and the influx of carefully selected and trained crews (of which the author was one) the Adler Geschwader formed its II Gruppe on 17 November 1939 and III Gruppe on 1 January 1940.

The complete KG 30 took part in the invasion of Denmark and Norway in April 1940 when the first attacks were made on shipping at sea. A month later, not less than eight Gruppen of Ju 88A bombers (KG 30, KG 51, and parts of KG 4 and LG 1) were available for the assault on the Low Countries and France but were not used operationally to any great extent (most of the bombing was done by He 111 and Do 17Z bombers). The acid test for the Ju 88As came during the Battle of Britain when, just as with other Luftwaffe bombers, their defensive armament and protection were found woefully inadequate. These operational experiences were hurriedly incorporated in the next variant, the Ju 88A-5, and the following Ju

88A-4 featuring the improved Jumo 211J engines and a new wing, in addition to augmented defensive armament and armour protection.

The Ju 88 went on to serve with distinction as a day and night bomber in all other theatres of war the Luftwaffe was involved in, from the Arctic to North Africa. The Ju 88 could also hold its own against enemy fighters far longer than other German bombers, particularly on the Eastern Front where the Luftwaffe bomber formations were gradually used in the support role instead of fulfilling their strategic tasks.

But it was as an anti-shipping bomber that the Ju 88 gained its most notable success during the first years of the war, the most prominent *Experten* being Werner Baumbach of KG 30 on the North Sea/Atlantic front and Joachim Helbig of I/LG 1* over the Mediterranean.

As related in this diary, Werner Baumbach met the author and persuaded him to become one of the 'experts' during one of his 'talent-spotting' visits to the subordinated units. Within a year, Baumbach had become an undisputed Ju 88 'ace' with more than 50,000 tons of shipping to his credit.**

Joachim Helbig was another unique Ju 88 pilot, a courageous leader and skilful dive bomber as shown by his successes against British shipping in the Mediterranean in 1941-42. Perhaps the most notable of these was the sinking of three Royal Navy destroyers (the HMS *Kipling, Lively* and *Jackal*) and the damage of a fourth (HMS *Jervis*) on 11 May 1942 by several Ju 88s led by Helbig: unlike merchantmen or larger warships, destroyers are a very difficult target to hit due to their small size, speed and agility.

The Ju 88s of KG 30 also played a significant part in raids on convoys to the Soviet Union until November 1942 when the unit was suddenly transferred to the Mediterranean area to join the 'Helbig Flyers', as they were known to the Allies. Beginning early 1942 the island fortress of Malta was another target for the Ju 88 dive

---

* LG 1 = Lehrgeschwader 1, Training and Instructional Wing, an elite formation. (Tr.)
** After several command appointments Werner Baumbach was selected to lead the special KG 200 formation in 1944. The author was asked to join KG 200 as Detachment commander in autumn 1944. (see *KG 200: The True Story* by P.W. Stahl/Jane's, 1981)

bombers, and they were also operational over North Africa by day and by night.

Meanwhile, suitably modified, the Ju 88 had also become the foremost Luftwaffe strategic reconnaissance aircraft (as Ju 88D series), had proved itself as a heavy day fighter over the Bay of Biscay, as a night intruder over the British Isles and elsewhere, and was beginning to make its mark as a night fighter. In this role the Ju 88 adaptations eventually proved so successful that they formed an increasingly larger proportion of the Luftwaffe night fighter force. For instance, of the 1,400 operational night fighters in the Luftwaffe inventory on 30 September 1944 no less than 739 were radar-equipped Ju 88 night fighters, the majority of the Ju 88G series. Some of the most successful Luftwaffe night fighter pilots preferred the Ju 88G to any other type, such as Oberst Helmut Lent (102 victories, killed in a flying accident on 7 October 1944) and Major Prince zu Sayn-Wittgenstein (83 victories, killed in action on 21 January 1944). In this capacity the Ju 88 served until the end of hostilities.

As a day bomber the basic Ju 88 was really past its prime by autumn 1942 but the Luftwaffe bomber crews had to make do for another year or so until more modern types began to reach the operational units. One of these was the Ju 188, already proposed as a Ju 88 development by Junkers engineers in 1940. Although a distinct advance over its forebear the Ju 188 was not accepted at the time, and when it finally was, the production was rather slow to get into its stride. Before that, there was also the Ju 88S high-speed bomber (and the parallel Ju 88T reconnaissance version), a streamlined basic Ju 88A without any unnecessary protruberances. Its more powerful engines made the Ju 88S the fastest Ju 88 variant produced, but only limited numbers were built and used operationally beginning early winter 1943.

By spring 1944 the Luftwaffe had lost its control of the air to the increasingly superior enemy strength on all fronts, and the delayed appearance of these new bombers made little impact on the situation. Within a few more months the fuel shortage caused by Allied precision bombing became chronic, and the Luftwaffe bomber force was run down in favour of the more essential fighters. The first jet-propelled Arado Ar 234 bombers too had shown their paces, and the Ju 188 was just too late. Its further development led to the Ju 388, evolved in several versions as a pressurised high-altitude reconnaissance aircraft, bomber and night fighter, but only a handful were completed before the capitulation.

The final design based on the Ju 88/188 family was the large four-engined Ju 488 high-altitude strategic reconnaissance bomber, but the two prototypes under construction in occupied France were destroyed by Allied bombing in 1944 before completion.

Ju 88A-4

First revised and modified version of the basic design. Intended for the 1,340/1,060 hp Jumo 211J engines but due to delays in engine development initial production series fitted with Jumo 211F units. Other major change was a new wing of increased span from 18.37 m (60 ft 3⅛ in) to 20.00 m (65 ft 7⅓ in) and, once the production began in autumn 1940, improved defensive armament. New internal fittings included extensive use of 4-9 mm armour plate protection for the crew, and forward bomb bay adapted to carry extra fuel tanks instead of bombs if required. RATO (rocket-assisted take-off) attachment point for overload/short airfield situations fitted as standard.

Data

2 × Junkers Jumo 211J-1 or J-2 inline engines, each rated at 1,340 hp for take-off and 1,060 hp at 5,180 m (17,000 ft). crew of 4.

Max speed 470 km/h (292 mph) at 5,300 m (17,390 ft). Time to 5,400 m (17,715 ft) – 23 min.

Service ceiling 8,200 m (26,900 ft). Normal range 1,790 km (1,112 miles) at 370 km/h (230 mph); max range 2,730 km (1,696 miles).

Weight empty equipped 9,860 kg (21,737 lb); norm loaded 12,100 kg (26,680 lb).

Span 20.00 m (65 ft 7⅓ in); length 14.40 m (47 ft 2¾ in); wing area 43.5 m² (586.6 ft²).

Armament (offensive): 500 kg (1,100 lb) bombs internally, plus max 2,000 kg (4,410 lb) bombs or mines externally.

Armament (defensive); basically 1 × 7.92 mm MG 15 or 1 × twin-barrel 7.92 mm MG 81Z semi-fixed forward (later 1 × 13 mm MG 131); 1 × 7.92 mm MG 15 or 1 × twin-barrel MG 81Z in ventral gondola facing aft, and 2 × 7.92 mm MG 81J machine guns in upper aft position; many Ju 88A-4s also fitted with two 7.92 mm MG 15 machine guns in beam positions. From summer 1941 bulged aft section of the cockpit canopy and new circular armour mountings for the twin upper guns, with variations. Some machines armed with 1 × 20 mm MG FF cannon firing forward in ventral gondola for anti-shipping attacks.

Subsequent numerous modifications of the A-series production aircraft were based on the Ju 88A-4, but did not necessarily enter service in the sequence of their sub-series numbers. They included the following:

Ju 88A-4/Torp torpedo-bomber adaptation of the standard bomber in 1942 and operational in the same year;

Ju 88A-6 balloon barrage destroyer fitted with a full-span balloon cable fender with cutting devices near the wingtips, withdrawn after a few operations in autumn 1940;

Ju 88A-6/U long-range maritime reconnaissance variant equipped with FuG 200 *Hohentwiel* ASV (air-surface vessel) search radar, operational over the Mediterranean in 1943;

Ju 88A-7 dual-control trainer modifications of standard A-5 airframes;

Ju 88A-8 bomber with balloon cable-cutting capability provided by the so-called *Kuto-Nase* cutting device built into the wing leading edge; small number completed in 1941;

Ju 88A-9 tropicalised bomber variant of the A-1 equipped with special water containers, sun blinds and desert survival kits. Completed before the A-8 version and operational in the Mediterranean area and North Africa in 1941-42;

Ju 88A-10 tropicalised bomber variant of the A-5 series; operational as A-9;

Ju 88A-11 tropicalised A-5, built as such from the outset. Operational in the Mediterranean area and North Africa in 1942-43;

Ju 88A-12 dual-control trainer modification of the A-4: deleted armament, ventral gondola and dive brakes;

Ju 88A-13 low-level attack modification of standard A-4 bomber. Deleted dive brakes and bomb sight, additional armour protection for the crew, engines and fuel tanks. Offensive armament comprised 500 kg (1100 lb) of small fragmentation bombs and 16 × 7.92 mm MG 17 machine guns in two weapon containers attached underwing. Operational on the Eastern Front;

Ju 88A-14 anti-shipping bomber with increased armour protection and Kuto-Nase wing leading edge equipment as standard; no dive brakes. Many machines armed with 1 × 20 mm MG FF cannon semi-fixed forward;

Ju 88A-15 bomber with a large external wooden bomb bay for max 3000 kg (6614 lb) bombs. Deleted ventral gun gondola, crew reduced to three man, defensive armament restricted to 2 × 7.92 mm MG 15 machine guns;

Ju 88A-16 dual-control trainer conversion of the A-14; only small number completed;

Ju 88A-17 torpedo-bomber built as such from the outset in 1942. 2 × 765 kg (1686 lb) LT F5b torpedoes on PVC racks under wing roots. Operational initially over the Mediterranean, then from Norway until the end of hostilities.

Index